OVER THE RAINBOW

BY

JA

GW00726955

**REFLECTING LIGHT ON PSYCHICS, MEDIUMS
AND THE SPIRITUAL NATURE OF LIFE**

Sincere Thanks
To those friends who helped
in the completion of this book.

ISBN 1 903151 279

Published by Island Light
Ryde, Isle of Wight

Printed by Olympia Press Ltd
36 Union Street, Ryde, IOW PO33 2LE

Cover illustration by Kevin Martin

CONTENTS

Foreword   4

1. How Psychics and Mediums Work   6
2. What You Should Expect from Psychics
and Mediums   19
3. The Difficulties Mediums Encounter and
Why They Sometimes Get Things Wrong.   25
4. Other Forms of Mediumship   30
5. How the Spirit Links with the Physical Body   37
6. The Spiritual Law of Cause and Effect,
Freewill and Suffering   47
7. Earth is a School, Reincarnation Another Term   55
8. The Myth of Religion   64
9. Genuine Spiritual Truths   70
10. All *Is* One, All *Is* God.   79
11. The Spiritual Realms of Progression   86

Conclusion   94
Glossary   96
Addresses   99

FOREWORD

When I was a young man a friend once asked me "what is the meaning of life?" although I doubt that he expected an answer. But now, following 23 years of serious study and investigation, and 37 years after first witnessing a demonstration of mediumship, I can at last attempt to provide one. (Sorry for the delay, John, I'm obviously a slow learner!).

I do so for all in this book form, not to show how 'clever' I am, for I am not, but because I understand that it is our responsibility in this life to share knowledge. And because it *is* your birthright, as the free spirit you truly are, to have this knowledge. By providing it I am merely doing what I consider the right thing. For I really do think it time that everyone knew the truth.

Many people in recent times have had their judgement clouded by the 'bureau of misinformation' as certain magicians and psychologists who have appeared on TV might be called. These magicians would have you believe that all psychics and mediums do is trickery, or the reading of body language in response to prompting dialogue. While the TV psychologists (and I know for a fact that these do not present the views of all in their profession) say all is a lie, that the mind and brain are one, and perish at physical death; and that anyone who thinks otherwise is deluding him or herself with wishful thinking. But they are badly mistaken.

Magicians *are* by trade tricksters and con artists, so those who have not looked beyond themselves, think the same of others. The TV psychologists are often and wrongly billed as 'paranormal experts'. But in relation to the true fact that we

4

all survive death, they blindfold themselves, for they refuse to look beyond a limited viewpoint. They cannot be experts in a subject they refuse to acknowledge exists. One day, when they open their minds, they will learn better.

Within, in the early chapters I present you with my composite understanding of psychics and mediums. While in the latter chapters I do my best to deal with 'the meaning of life', with my understanding on the spiritual nature of life. I have endeavoured to include something on every aspect that I consider important. Although there are whole books written on much of the information that I, in moderate length chapters, have covered, available to those keen to learn in even greater depth and detail, including some of my own. I do not claim infallibility, for just like everyone else upon this planet, I still have much to learn.

I hope that what I am able to share will prove itself a useful addition to your spiritual understanding. If you find it hard to believe or accept certain points, it is naturally your right to either dismiss or reserve judgement. If you believe in nothing this too is your right. All I ask is your indulgence and consideration. It is not for me to *tell* you anything; I can only say what I have learned, and what I *believe* to be truth. It befalls you, if you so choose, to seek your own truth. For the burden of proof is with each individual. We should all use our own reasoning faculties to investigate, deduce, and establish what is fair to call our own truth. There is no shortcut to wisdom, but knowledge and truth must come first, as stepping-stones upon the pathway. If you need it to be so, I hope that this book will be as a stepping-stone to you.

The terms used in this book are in general self-explanatory and quite easy to follow. However, those who are totally unfamiliar with the subject matter may find it useful to refer to the glossary located near the end of the book. Happy reading.

Chapter 1

HOW PSYCHICS & MEDIUMS WORK

PSYCHICS

Many people seem to use the term "psychic" for all sensitives. When in strict terms it is most useful to understand the difference between a psychic and a medium.

Psychics make use of what to most of us would be a heightened sensitivity. They consciously or unconsciously open their auric senses and receive vibrational information. This sometimes embraces what is termed "psychometry", which involves handling something belonging to the person for whom they intend to deliver a "reading". Objects, all matter, can be imprinted with vibrations, particularly those worn or handled frequently. Although most that practice psychometry say they prefer an object that is metallic, such as a ring, necklace, bracelet or wristwatch. For it is considered that these "register" a stronger vibration – making the vibrations (theoretically at least) easier to decode or decipher. Just as a stronger TV or radio signal produces a better and clearer picture or sound.

The observant reader might realise that since it is the energy of the person (imprinted on the object) that is actually being "read", an object is not strictly necessary. This is true. Many psychics – knowingly or unknowingly – can "pick-up" on the vibrations of another without any form of physical touch. In the same way that all of us have sensed when someone is approaching us from behind. Or even sensed when someone was staring at us from a moderate distance (across a room etc.).

What allows us to sense someone in these two examples is our own personal energy field. Firstly, our aura (energy field) can be larger and more sensitive than one might imagine. So when someone approaches you from behind his or her energy touches your energy, and you sense that they are there. Across a room, or even across a street, someone staring will project energy, most generally without realising that they are doing so and, if projected sufficiently, again this will touch your own energy field and alert you. We are all capable of receiving and projecting energy, and without realising do so regularly.

The important thing to remember is that someone who is purely psychic cannot give you a message from anyone in the spiritual realms. If their psychic ability is well developed however they may be capable of reading much about you from your energy vibrations, whether utilising psychometry or simply by concentrating upon you (again, this will cause their energy to temporarily link with your energy). Distance actually presents no obstacle to such energy links, which is why a psychic can be somewhere far away and still link with your energy. Sometimes, particularly for a postal reading, a psychic might ask for a photograph or a lock of your hair etc., the photograph will act for them as a focal point for concentration, while your lock of hair, having registered your vibrations, will assist them to "attune" to you.

To anyone new to such investigations this may sound far-fetched, but it is nonetheless perfectly true. It is the reason why secret service agencies around the world have been utilising the abilities of psychics. For at the top end of the scale of ability a highly proficient psychic will be able to "tune-in" to the recent thoughts and activities of your life. For example, perhaps where you are located, what you have been observing, whom you have met and what you might have discussed, and much more. If they have a particular question about you an answer may even present itself to them. So a top notch psychic, and I am not suggesting that many, if any, reach a standard where all and any sought information will be forthcoming to them, can be most receptive and glean much information from someone's energy field.

How much is stored in our energy? Well, quite literally, everything. From thoughts and emotions to actions and ideas. All is there. But that which is particularly forthcoming to a psychic is strong impressions, especially those more recent. So anything, which makes a deep impression in your life, will be more readily accessible. This is why strong emotional impressions of love, rejection, joy and pain, are so often "picked up" by a psychic. It is similar to what I said earlier for psychometry – an object regularly worn would absorb a stronger impression. Likewise, a stronger and intensely felt emotion or reaction will send a stronger signal into one's own energy field. It must register there because your energy field is you. It is part of your spiritual essence. You cannot "escape" yourself. All in your life is registered within your spiritual essence. Consciously you may forget, but nothing, even of the slightest relevance, is ever totally lost.

Psychics are of course not all "top notch" sensitives, far from it. Many fall well below this description. In fact, as indicated earlier by my reference to all of us having at one time or another felt the presence of someone approaching us from behind, it can be gathered that to an extent we are *all* psychic.

We are all spiritual beings with our own aura. Each of us is capable of using our spiritual faculties to the degree that we have progressed. As in all endeavours of life practise will improve. A would be artist who wishes to paint a landscape will not find it very easy when they first try. But if they have such ability within them, gradually, perhaps with help, guidance, training and practise they will reveal their ability. In such a scenario we would not expect all to produce landscapes of the same quality. In other words some will find that they have greater aptitude or ability than others. Psychic ability (and mediumship) is likewise no different; some will find within themselves a finer aptitude than others.

MEDIUMS

A true mental medium (that is clairvoyant, clairaudient or clairsentient, or a mixture) is a go between, a link, and a translator of telepathic transmissions from those who are residents of the spirit realms. They are called "mental mediums" because what they receive comes through the faculty of mind, and contrary to what some might mischievously try to imply, is in no way a reflection of their state of mental health!

Clairvoyance

The word means "clear seeing". It is the most commonly used term to infer mediumship, and is perhaps the principle way that many mediums receive. In an attempt to communicate a spirit person will send telepathic images to a medium in the hope that firstly, they will see them clearly as an impression upon their "minds eye", and that secondly they will be able to translate what they receive.

As you may gather, we are already asking much.

Clairaudience

The word means "clear hearing". Some mediums are better able to receive telepathic thought transmissions, rather than images. So naturally, if this is the case, a spirit person will transmit their thoughts and hope that these, via the subconscious mind of the medium, will register and instantly be relayed to the conscious thoughts of the medium.

Again we are asking much, for the medium has to isolate

from their own thoughts that which they receive. Although some, the fortunate few, being blessed with a degree of physical mediumship qualities, are able to have the incoming thoughts enhanced by means of ectoplasm.

Clairsentience

The word means "clear feeling". Many mediums work in this way in addition to either or both clairvoyance and clairaudience. While some receive communication only in this way. If the spirit person knows that a medium can only receive in this way, rather than telepathically transmitting images or thoughts, they will send feelings. This may not sound as potentially fruitful, but a medium that is accomplished at receiving and interpreting in this way can still be most accurate in what they pass as a message. Much, as you would expect, will depend upon how well developed the medium is, how intuitively receptive they are at understanding the message behind or contained within the feelings.

The method of spirit transmission in image, thought, or feeling, as I have said can reflect the receptivity of the medium. However, it is also possible that the spirit persons themselves will prefer a particular method of transmission. For their personalities do not suddenly change upon passing. So one who was good at verbal communication may prefer to telepathically 'speak' their thoughts. While some, because they may find it more difficult to telepathically picture or phrase their thoughts, may prefer sending feelings. (Animals too, can transmit feelings). It should also be borne in mind that there is no instant understanding gained upon passing, all needs to be learned, and it is not necessarily easy to telepathically send thoughts, even if you were good at conversation when upon earth.

From Psychic to Medium

A medium can be utilising psychic ability, along with mediumship. So it is often difficult to be sure how much of each is actually being used.

Since we are all spiritual beings, we each have the potential to display, and develop further, any natural psychic or mediumistic capabilities. Many will deny any such capability and say that they have no psychic ability, let alone any mediumistic ability. Yet it is commonplace to experience my earlier example of "knowing" when someone is approaching from behind, or staring at you, which are both displays of psychic intuitiveness.

I have written a brief checklist to show a range of psychic through to mediumistic abilities from minor psychic to the heights of mediumship. Each level embraces those below, so those who exhibit abilities to level four will also be capable of experiencing at levels one, two and three, and so forth. Not necessarily in the identical way that I have listed, for these are only examples; so some may have alternative abilities to those quoted, indeed you may think of other examples to add.

Purely Psychic

Level 1. As previously mentioned, without seeing or hearing, you sense when someone is approaching. When you are being stared at you "feel" this and turn to face the person.

Level 2. You sense when the telephone is about to ring, and instinctively may know who will be calling and perhaps why. You suddenly think of someone, often someone you have not seen for some time, and either they telephone, visit, or you meet them on the street.

Level 3. Those at this level may be aware that they have some ability more than the average person, although they may choose to tell only family and close friends. They will, for example, be able to read the tealeaves or some other tool, even if in a limited way. Or similarly they will occasionally use Playing, Tarot or other cards.

Level 4. Next are those who more readily admit to their ability with one or other of the aforementioned tools, and are more inclined to use them. So they may take great delight in giving mini readings for anyone who is interested. In addition or alternative to the tools listed, they may embrace psychometry.

Level 5. We now reach the level when some of those with sufficient psychic ability may decide that they can use this to earn a little money. How much, depends upon their confidence, desire, needs and conscience. At this level a prop will most certainly be used, whether a crystal ball or more commonly Tarot or similar cards, Rune stones, or one of many other choices utilised around the world. A reading from someone at this level may be a bit of a hit or miss affair, for each day the ability they have to attune to your energies can fluctuate. Also, their energies may or may not be capable of *finely* attuning to your energies, although in most cases they will have some success.

Level 6. Again, this level will embrace such as the Tarot card reader. But, at the top end of the purely psychic scale, some are more proficient, and more in control of their ability. They are therefore more capable of attuning to the energies of a range of sitters. Experience will naturally assist their ability to provide an accurate reading; for this will have taught them how to interpret what they are able to receive; those adept at interpreting can be proven most accurate. While a genuine willingness to be of service does make a difference, for those of a sympathetic nature are more likely to achieve a finer vibratory link.

A Mixture of Psychic and Mediumistic

Level 7. At this level we begin the overlap between psychic ability and mediumship. Many at this level will be offering their services to the public, but will most likely call themselves a psychic or a clairvoyant psychic. A sitting with someone at this level of development will provide all the information obtained by a proficient psychic along with a little input from perhaps one or two close relatives from the spiritual realms. As a gauge let us say that the reading will be 90% psychic and 10% mediumistic.

Level 8. To gauge in absolute terms we could have a level for every percentage point and then some, so from hereon you can assume that there are many levels (or sub levels) between each one that I have listed. So for the sake of simplicity, let us say that those at this level use 75% psychic ability and 25% mediumistic ability.

In addition to psychically obtained information they may achieve a tentative link with relatives who might give a few family names that you recognise, along with their love. Any other information may well lack clarity, and you may find that they have to ask a number of questions, which will hopefully enable you to understand the communication. For the input that they are receiving may be symbolic and fragmented, and therefore very difficult for them to interpret.

Level 9. Let us now jump straight to the middle ground. Someone who may simply call himself or herself a medium or clairvoyant, but who still utilises 50% psychic intuitiveness or receptivity along with 50% mediumship. Here we can get a very accurate psychic reading, but the mediumship, albeit better than someone at the level below, may still lack clarity. They may get a number of names that are recognisable, but they may also get many that are not. They may pass a reasonably accurate description of a close relative or friend, although it may lack some element of precision, perhaps it will be most accurate apart from one detail. Such a sitting would be satisfactory to a point, but would most likely leave you unsure as to whether a link was truly made, or whether guesswork was involved.

Level 10. From the level below to this and beyond you will find a vast number of psychics and mediums with receptivity that is variable between mediocre and occasional spot-on aspects. Although we are now nearing the level of more dedicated mediumship, those at this level will still use psychic intuitiveness but typically this will account for only say 25% of their reading, while 75% will involve mediumship (although not necessarily of outstanding accomplishment). They would almost certainly call themselves a medium, or if being more descriptive may choose to use the title clairvoyant, clairaudient, or clairsentient, perhaps with medium tagged on at the end.

Here any reading may start with a little psychically gleaned information, to help get the mediumship attuned, but will (hopefully) quickly develop to pass information obtained from at least one, sometimes several, spirit communicators.

Pure Mediumship

Level 11. Although many mediums use their psychic abilities to get them attuned or as a starting link, those whom we can put towards the top of our list really do attempt to use mediumship at all private sittings (or public demonstrations). They will normally call themselves a medium, but once again the accuracy of the communications they receive can vary greatly.

At the lower level of pure mediumship, if an accuracy measure could be applied, it may find a number achieving say 30% confirmation to their communications. A good percentage of what they attempt to relate would be found vague, for two reasons. One is because the medium is not fully attuned to the spirit communicator, so the incoming telepathic message is difficult to receive in precise terms, not that precision is ever easy. The second reason is because even if the message is well received, it is still a telepathic thought transmission, often in symbolic imagery, so the spirit communicator relies upon the medium to be sufficiently aware or intuitive to act as interpreter. If the medium misunderstands a symbolic communication things can become most confusing. If both reasons are a problem, then we really will struggle to make sense of what the spirit communicator is attempting to transmit.

Level 12. As we move up the mediumship levels the successful reception and onward communication to the sitter improves in quality or accuracy. Let us introduce a variable and say that at this level the "success" rate reaches 60-70% (to remind you, there are many mediums who are somewhere between each level, and perhaps especially so between levels 11 and 12). We will call "success" a communication that is readily accepted as accurate. At this level success reaches a standard that I think we can quite fairly call good-to-very good mediumship. (Not that one wishes to act as judge, but we, like those in spirit when their thoughts are translated, are limited to language and understandable terms).

Level 13+. Hereon, mediumship that achieves a success rate of 75% and above can be deemed excellent. With the top end of this scale (80%-100%), achieved by very few mediums throughout history. All those who achieve the development of mediumship are the ambassadors of spirit, for attempting to demonstrate proof of eternal life, we should be proud of them. For often it has taken courage; and always it demands personal commitment, perseverance, and in the vast majority of cases a willingness to sacrifice. Which can include aspects of their personal life due to the amount of time given for travelling and demonstrating, as well as financially. For contrary to what some believe, the majority receive remuneration that is the equivalent of far less than the minimum wage, if anything at all, for some merely ask for travel expenses.

My "levels", as I have tried to emphasise, are of course just rough guides. As may be gathered, not only are there many ranges of ability (levels) into which we could attempt to pigeon hole psychics and mediums, but that even these will have many variables. For instance, someone might attempt to pass 75% or more information as spirit messages, when in fact they may inadvertently be deluding themselves, and may only be achieving a much smaller percentage of communication. The rest of the information they pass may be psychically gleaned, without them even realising so.

Another important variable that should be noted by all that attend for private readings, or public demonstrations, is that the atmosphere generated by individual or group can and does have an impact upon the receptivity of the medium.

A medium is a receiving station, one capable of attunement with higher frequencies of vibration. Just like a TV or radio, if their attunement is not fine their reception is poor or non-existent.

Mediums are not mechanical. Their receptive attunement is associated with their aura through which the telepathic imagery, thoughts and/or feelings pass. These fields of energy are not isolated from sitters or the world at large. Their energy fields, indeed our own energy fields too, are constantly being bombarded with vibrations from many sources. Not from the spiritual dimensions alone, but also from the physical world. Much of this we are largely immune to, for it is mostly familiar to our energy vibrations. But when a medium prepares to demonstrate and link with those from the spirit side of life, their sensitivity and vibrations are heightened and naturally become more aware of thoughts and feelings. This is as it should be to receive input from those in spirit. However, it also makes them more vulnerable to the thoughts, feelings and emotions of the sitter(s).

In this state of "heightened awareness" if one or more of the sitters are of a hostile nature they can interfere quite easily with communication. For such an attitude creates its own adverse frequency. To the medium it is like trying to align an aerial in a positive direction, while the sitter(s) in the very same air space align one in a negative direction. The result, as it would be with a TV or radio signal, is that it causes interference.

So when a sitter attends with a negative "Prove it to me", or "I know this is a trick" or "I don't believe but the wife dragged me along" attitude, the signal they send out literally is a counter-productive vibration. This makes communication more difficult, and in consequence less precise or accurate. To the medium the problems caused amount to the same as trying to view a flickering, distorted, badly faded or blank screen, listen to a scratched, jumping or fragmented disc or tape, or feel what a spirit person wished you to feel while also being bombarded by negative feelings by the sitter(s).

This is not to say that all less perfect sittings are down to the sitter(s), for mediums, just like all of us, can have off days. They may be physically tired, stressed or strained, so their personal batteries may be weakened, and as a result may have difficulty concentrating and tuning in, which can make reception more difficult, distorted or fragmented.

However, on the positive side, from personal experience, I can say that if you give mediumship a fair chance and always approach with an open mind, later if not sooner, you will find a medium capable of assuring you of survival.

Chapter 2

WHAT YOU SHOULD EXPECT FROM
PSYCHICS & MEDIUMS

PSYCHICS

As you will have gathered from reading chapter one, someone who is purely psychic will glean all the information they might pass to you at a sitting from your own energy field. To reiterate, none of this information will be from anyone resident in the spiritual realms, all will be from you.

Whether they use an object, as with psychometry, or a crystal ball or tarot cards etc. will reflect their preferred method of attuning to your energies, and sensitising (using their own sensitivity to interpret) what they receive.

So what should you expect from a psychic? Well, typically they will tell you things you largely know and can confirm as correct or accurate. For instance, they may start with aspects of your life that are more to the forefront of your thoughts and emotions. You may be considering a change of employment, home, or have other financial concerns which they will mention. Or relationship satisfaction, worry or problems might be forthcoming. These may of course be expanded upon in suitable detail that is personally applicable to you. While issues in relation to family and friends might also be dealt with in due course, because what you have learned from others will also be registered within your own personal energy field.

What they may go on to perceive (as chapter one, dependent upon the sensitivity and ability of the psychic) may be more deeply held thoughts. Such as those that reveal your inner character - what sort of person you truly are, perhaps also any fears and phobias, and examples of things you may particularly enjoy or dislike. Additionally, it is quite conceivable that things you may temporarily have forgotten, may be revealed. This is possible because the *greater you*, embraced within your energy vibrations, will have stored everything with perceivable value of which you have experience. For your energies, or energy fields, are of spirit, and infallible, although in the fullness of time irrelevant memories may fade.

So, you might say "why bother having a sitting with a psychic, if they can only tell me what at some level I already know". Well, at the level of psychic perception so far mentioned, the sitting serves no purpose other than demonstrating that such psychic ability exists. If you seek communication with someone residing in the spiritual realms this will not be forthcoming.

However, since we are dealing with variables, once more, as mentioned in chapter one, if the psychic is sensitive enough, useful guidance might, in more ways than one, also be forthcoming. Firstly, straying slightly from the purely psychic, it is possible that thoughts and ideas (guidance) might filter into the thoughts of the psychic from another mind, albeit without the psychic being aware from whence the thoughts originate. As we move through the "levels" of sensitivity the chance of awareness grows. But leaving this aside, there is a second possibility why guidance might be forthcoming, even via a purely psychic link. It is because your energy field, at a higher vibration in your being, itself contains spiritual knowledge pertaining to you. Once more we are dealing with the sensitivity and ability of each individual psychic. If they are able to glean information from your higher vibrations, often referred to as the "higher mind", which is beyond normal consciousness, and in possession of knowledge such as your life purpose, direction or plan, then guidance of a much higher calibre might, potentially, become known to them.

I have used the word "potentially" in an attempt to emphasise that although a psychic *might* glean such information, to find one of such calibre, in my opinion, is rare. For, as my "levels" indicate, the finer the quality the more inclined to develop mediumship. However, it is also fair to say that not all psychics, no matter how good, have the potential to develop mediumistically.

A further point for consideration, is that even if what you receive is information already known to you, this too may have value, for it may act as a mirror, allowing you to view or review aspects or circumstances of your life. For if something in your energy field immediately "jumps out" to a psychic, then in some way it may be something you need to take another look at. Perhaps it concerns something you have not given enough thought to or fully dealt with. For sometimes what lies on the surface of your aura are unresolved issues. Not always, but sometimes. So when a psychic mentions them, you may need to review your position and perhaps take some action in relation to them. While issues that have been dealt with and resolved satisfactorily are, if they are revealed at all, more likely to come through as past data.

So although the purely psychic will not receive information from those in the spiritual realms, they can be most informative and useful, and play their own part in furthering understanding of life.

What you should expect from psychics is therefore dependent upon their individual sensitivity and ability to interpret the vibrational information they receive. Whether they receive via "clairvoyant-style" pictorial imagery or "clairsentient-style" sensitivity – it is still largely their ability to translate, to make sense of what they receive, that will either satisfy, frustrate, or mystify you.

MEDIUMS

So what should you expect from a medium? Well, if I was to put this in one brief sentence, it would be, "proof of survival". For this is the primary agenda undertaken by most mediums. Although, 'the philosophy of spirit' imparted by many mediums at public meetings before demonstrating is also of great importance.

To provide proof of survival, a medium will endeavour to forge a telepathic link with whoever comes forward from the spiritual realms to communicate with you. This will have nothing to do with any desire on behalf of the medium or yourself. It will be a freewill decision made by the spirit communicator, for it is always their choice whether or not to return and attempt to communicate; nobody can ever summon or "call them up", it simply does not work that way. For they are as free as you or I to choose when and whom they visit, with vast numbers living in realms where they enjoy far greater freedom of expression than is available to many upon earth.

Most often the returning person (or "spirit" as they tend to be called) will be a relative or loved one, otherwise a friend (or occasionally a guide or helper). Whoever it is, in a typical sitting they will attempt to identify themselves. They may, if the medium is clairaudient, give their name, or identify themselves as Mother or Father etc. If the medium is able to clairvoyantly see them, they will most likely do their best to describe them to you. While if the medium is purely clairsentient, the communicator will most likely try to impart to them the 'feeling' of their relationship to you.

The communicator is likely to follow this with further information to confirm their identity that, if successful, should at very least go part way to proving their continued existence. Perhaps the communicator will mention some habits or hobbies they had while upon earth. Or they may mention some memories they have, and hopefully those which you will share.

Having established that you recognise the communicator, before ending the communication it is usual for the communicator to let you know if they have any particular reason, other than proving their survival, for returning to visit you. This can simply be to reassure you that they are fine, that they still love you, and to show you that they are still taking an interest in your life and well-being. Or, it might additionally be to offer some guidance on a particular issue current in your life. However, it is important to know and remember that guidance is only to advise, they may seek to help you, but you should only take advice that you personally are in agreement with – as you might have done when they were in physical form. Passing to the spiritual realms will not have transformed them overnight into gurus of wisdom. They will for some time be very much as they were when upon earth, and they should not seek to *tell* you what to do. Your life is for you to live.

The philosophy of spirit is simple to comprehend. The most important aspect of this I can also summarise in a brief sentence, that is, "cause and effect". Biblically this is described as "as you sow so shall you reap". In other words, what you give out in life reverberates back to you. Not necessarily quickly, although this can happen, but eventually, in eternity, it is an inescapable consequence. Given time and opportunity, it would be hoped that a medium would, in addition to proof of survival, be able to teach you this. If not, do not despair, for I have more to say on this subject in later chapters.

Finally, to conclude this chapter, there are a couple of things that a genuine medium should not do. Firstly, they should not expect you to answer any questions other than to reply yes, no, or don't know etc. Secondly, they should not claim any kind of infallibility. If they fail in either respect, it is a sure indication that they are either a novice medium or one from the lower levels of development, or worse still, that they are in fact a confidence trickster, and not a medium. So please do be aware of this before you part with any money, particularly if you consider their fee excessive. If you do not know where to look for a genuine medium seek assistance from the SNU (see addresses) or a trustworthy word of mouth recommendation.

Chapter 3

THE DIFFICULTIES MEDIUMS ENCOUNTER & WHY THEY SOMETIMES GET THINGS WRONG

When one thinks of the different "levels" of mediumship I have already covered in Chapter One, I am sure that any reasonable person would be quite surprised to find a medium who did not on at least some occasions encounter difficulties. Even the better exponents of mediumship are, like all of us, prone to "off days". So it would be surprising to find any that did not on occasions have problems with their reception, and by consequence at least here and there "get things wrong" or make mistakes. The lower their level, the more so; and I mean no disrespect when I say so. For we should always remember that mediums are literally attempting to communicate with people who are living in a different dimension of eternal life.

In many ways we should be astounded that some are able to receive and interpret as well as they do. So with this in mind let me summarise and expand upon the difficulties they encounter, and why they sometimes get things wrong. As well as why psychic or mediumistic predictions so often fail.

Firstly, to reiterate we must consider the different standards of mediumship, particularly in regard to the more popularly used "gifts" of clairvoyance, clairaudience and clairsentience, for these can vary considerably. Some mediums are more naturally sensitive, and are sometimes psychic or mediumistic from childhood. While others do not recognise their potential until adulthood, and from whatever age this happens, gradually develop their sensitivity; and by practise, patience and perseverance, usually through development circles with meditation, enhance their receptivity and learn to interpret the communications they receive.

Yet even if every potential medium were to put all of their spare time into enhancing their sensitivity and learning how best to interpret the often symbolised telepathic communications they receive, and these are symbolised because of the difficulty of long-drawn communications, even then, some would be more finely attuned than others. Just as when we start school, despite all sitting through the same initial lessons, some by nature will have a greater aptitude for English, some for Mathematics, while others feel more comfortable with music, artistic or even physical or athletic pursuits.

While sometimes we find we have absolutely no inclination for a particular subject or pursuit. For example, many people openly admit to being hopeless at the artistic discipline of drawing or painting. Mediumship is no different. Potentially we can all develop it, just as we can all pick up a pencil and draw, but not all will reach a standard to make pursuit desirable. Likewise with singing, some have no aptitude, and "if they have to" may if they attend a church mutter along with a hymn, while others will reach the heights of their potential and become famous singers. So we must expect to find some less sensitively attuned mediums, who will not be able to channel through particularly descriptive or detailed communications from those in the spirit dimensions of life.

For instance, to reach the level of sensitive receptivity required to receive surnames and addresses on a regular basis is achieved by few these days. Perhaps because there are now just too many distractions put in front of us. For in days prior to TV and radio, when there were fewer distractions, by all accounts there were more mediums of the calibre to communicate surnames and addresses. But to remind readers mediumship, or "inter-dimensional communication", which it truly is, is not often achieved without great effort and commitment. No more than it is easy to become a top-level artist, singer, or for that matter, furniture maker. Very few in this present age are willing to devote their time to a long drawn-out occupational apprenticeship, let alone to one as precarious, and generally with little financial reward, as mediumship. If we feel the urge to complain about the standards of mediumship, then there is really only one answer, and that is to have a go at developing it ourselves. Then, we might better appreciate the difficulties.

I come now to the subject of why so many predictions from those in the spiritual realms fail. Firstly, we must remember that relatives who communicate are often on, let us say, an elementary level of the astral world. At this level, which we are told is a near replica to the earth plane, they often know little if any more than the person to whom they are passing a message, so any predictions, or what a medium perceives as a prediction, is often meaningless.

What can happen is that the relative or friend merely wants to show you that they have been taking an interest in what is happening in your day-to-day life. Or they might wish to make a suggestion, or pass advice in the same manner, as they might have liked to do when upon earth. They may even be privy to certain events in your life that may appear to be leading to a certain conclusion, and they may say so, either as a misguided or otherwise prediction. Or perhaps, and I would like to think more generally, as a forecast of a likely outcome. But, via *some* mediums (not all), this may come across as a "sure" prediction. For again we are dealing with the level, attunement and experience of the medium, and as you will gather this can vary greatly. Of course, the medium passing the message may be under the impression that the prediction is a certainty. For mediums in general have to learn to trust what they receive, to know the difference between a communication and their own imagination, and sometimes this trust may inadvertently encourage them to suggest that such and such a prediction will (sometimes "eventually") come to fruition. So because of either the medium, or indeed because of the communicators desire to believe that what they "foresee" will occur, the message is passed as a sure prediction. But, what the recipient should be receiving is often no more than the opinion of the friend or relative.

Unfortunately, as so often is the case upon earth, the relative or friend is not in possession of all the facts, and does not fully understand the intricacies that go to make up the mind of even a close loved one. So they get it wrong. The person does not act, react, or proceed as the spirit communicator anticipated. However, having said all this, there are occasions when accurate predictions are made.

Higher guides, your real guides, are less likely to offer predictions. Especially concerning your physical day-to-day life, for they have total respect for your freewill. So without good reason they will rarely make predictions, for by the very nature of the word, a prediction is most generally a "guess". Although if you have concerns and ask for guidance, particularly of a spiritual nature, a guide may offer guidance or an opinion, but they will leave you to make your own decisions.

So in conclusion for this chapter, it can be gathered and hopefully appreciated that mediumistic communication, which to remind you is "inter-dimensional communication" (a description I have deliberately chosen to highlight the complexity), is not a one hundred per cent reliable link. It is subject to a number of problems and potential pitfalls. But this does not mean that it is anything but genuine.

I feel that it is important that people should be more aware of the difficulties, for then they can better understand why some messages are less detailed or accurate than others. No one is really to blame. Personally, I would not blame an over zealous spirit relative for trying to pass on information, whether misunderstood by the medium or wrongly anticipated by themselves. For I am sure that they and the mediums endeavour to do their best, but like us, are only human. So errors are bound to occur, just as they do upon the earth plane – and we, when we receive a message, can be guilty of misunderstanding or jumping to wrong conclusions too!

This is why many mediums do not like making or passing on predictions, and prefer to stick to survival evidence, although, bearing in mind what I said earlier in this chapter, you can perhaps also better understand why even this information can, on occasions, go awry. If you still need proof of survival, then perseverance is the key, for in time, even allowing for the difficulties, enough accurate information, which cannot be disputed and can only have come from discarnate relatives or friends, will be forthcoming to satisfy even the most hardened sceptic.

Chapter 4

OTHER FORMS OF MEDIUMSHIP

Mediumship can take a number of forms; in addition to those already mentioned these can include trance, physical, psychic/ spiritual art, and healing mediumship. Whole books have been written in relation to these aspects of mediumship. I mention them purely in brief, so as to cover as many aspects from what I have learned during my investigations and studies. All are fascinating in their own right; if one is of particular interest to you, then please do seek out further and more detailed information. The more you learn the more you will find there is to learn. Other aspects, avenues and ways in which to view, consider and sometimes use a subject will naturally reveal themselves to the open-minded seeker. They function as follows.

Trance Mediumship
Trance mediumship, in a sense, appears as a more direct form of communication than clairvoyance, clairaudience or clairsentience. A spirit person, who is usually a guide, although occasionally a relative or friend, with permission of the medium, whose physical body and senses they use, is able to communicate in a seemingly direct fashion. The spirit person is able to transfer their thoughts telepathically so that they engage the vocal cords of the medium, and these are spoken as in normal speech. In order to achieve such a link, the communicator needs to be on a similar frequency to the medium, in the same way that TV or radio in order to work needs the transmitter and receiver set at the same frequency.

To assist this link the medium will calm their mind and, if sufficiently relaxed, their consciousness will either temporarily vacate their physical body, or remain in a withdrawn non-active state, in a fashion similar to that which we all experience whilst sleeping. This allows for a state of spirit attunement, so that a mind-to-mind link can be achieved. When ready, through the unconscious and subconscious mind of the medium, the thoughts of the spirit communicator can flow to the mind of the medium.

Trance mediumship, at its best, can be wonderful to witness. Excellent communication is possible in this way, and many wonderful books have been produced. For example the teachings of Silver Birch, White Feather, Red Cloud and White Eagle are amongst many spirit realm philosophers whose wisdom has been received through deep trance communication and reproduced in print. Such guides as these, understanding that proof of their former earthly life is often impossible to prove, always ask that you accept only what sits right with your own reason or inner feeling.

Physical Mediumship

Physical mediumship can take many forms. The wonderful thing about it, as the name implies, is that it can be witnessed with physical senses. So in an ideal scenario if you are lucky enough to witness a top demonstration you may find that a friend or relative will actually materialise in physical form, so that you can see, hear and with permission even touch them.

Unfortunately, very few are lucky enough to find themselves in the position to sit in such a demonstration – or more generally, circle. For such circles are nearly always "closed shops". This is not because what is developed is in any way trickery. It is because of the delicate nature of the task of blending energies. This is entirely undertaken from the spirit side of life, but they are reliant upon having suitable sitters present. First they need someone with the right spiritual 'make-up', the right harmonics in their aura, to function as the physical medium, then, they need an harmonious atmosphere to be generated by those who sit with the physical medium, this is most important.

Energies can then be blended and built, more commonly using a substance called ectoplasm that is mostly drawn from the physical medium ('new energy' sources have also more recently been spirit developed), to produce phenomena. Materialisation of complete spirit beings is the ideal 'top of the tree' aim. But there are many other forms of physical phenomena, which can often be witnessed by all present.

These can include part materialisation, when such as the head or hand is shown. The whole spirit person is really present, but when enough energy and subsequent build material is not available this is all that can be materialised. Direct voice is perhaps next best, when through a spirit-constructed voice box or earth trumpet the visiting spirits can effectively speak direct to those present. Even though in reality the spirit communicator's thoughts telepathically reach the mind of the medium then pass through a cord constructed of ectoplasm (or energy) to the voice box or trumpet where it transforms to physically audible sound waves. This may sound technical, and from the spirit side of life it probably is, but at the physical level what can be received is a voice that often is very much a perfect replica of the communicator's genuine voice when upon earth. Once all is in place conversation is as instantaneous as upon earth, for thought travels faster than the speed of light.

Other examples of physical phenomena include levitation, apports (the materialisation of objects), spirit lights appearing and 'dancing' around, tables or objects being moved by unseen spirit people, and much more. I call physical mediumship the ultimate proof. It cannot be demonstrated to everyone, because of the need for a harmonious atmosphere; the anti "it is all a trick" brigades will be least likely to witness, because the energies they project would certainly be counter productive.

The Mediumship of Psychic or Spiritual Art

Psychic art, as more traditionally called, or Spiritual art as perhaps more befitting, is most commonly the portrait drawing (or painting) of spirit people (or animals). Quite often the portraits are of known relatives or friends, and are recognised by the intended recipient.

Occasionally, other spirit friends are drawn, guides or helpers for instance. Although the drawing of such personalities may not represent proof of survival, they can be pleasing and reassuring to receive, especially by someone seeking to work more closely with their spirit guides or helpers. A name or description may also be given before or at a later date by a completely different medium, to confirm the authenticity of the drawing.

Such inspired artists can work in different ways. Some are capable artists in their own right and are able to draw the portrait of the spirit they clairvoyantly see. While others have no obvious artistic ability and find themselves either guided by unseen hand or during the process inspired or overshadowed as in the early stages of trance.

In whichever way inspired, the numbers of drawings with photographic evidence of accuracy later produced by numerous (thousands) of recipients is undeniable by all but the most closed-minded sceptic.

Healing Mediumship

We are all alike at birth. That is to say, we each in essence have the same type of spiritual makeup. We each have the same number of finer energy bodies and chakras. We have the same connection to divinity or creation, and to the spiritual and life force energies. Therefore, to degree, we can all call upon this power and channel healing energies.

However, because we are all unique individuals, some have progressed further upon certain pathways than others. This is reflected within our energy vibratory status. Those who have progressed further along pathways that enhance the channelling of spiritual healing energies will naturally be more likely to achieve better results with its practice. This does not necessarily mean they are more progressed in all ways. For life offers many pathways.

Contact Healing

Contact healing, as the name implies, can occur when the healing channel, generally called the "healer", and recipient are physically together, usually in a room or hall. Physical touch is often made, although it is not strictly necessary. For healing flows in chain fashion, and this is usually described as from spirit, through spirit, to spirit. Which means, the energies that flow from the spiritual dimensions in response to prayerful request (from spirit), pass through the aura (finer energy bodies) of the healer (through spirit), to the aura of the recipient (to spirit). So if the healer makes contact with the aura of the recipient, without physical bodily touch, this is nonetheless sufficient.

As can be read in later chapters, we are all composite beings, and what effects one aspect to greater or lesser degree affects all. There are many books, including my own small book, on spiritual healing, so I am being most brief herein with my information upon it. Effectively, spiritual healing energies are intended to re-harmonise or restore balance to the finer energy bodies, to the chakras, and as necessary and whenever possible by natural consequence to the physical body.

Spiritual healing energies can on occasions come direct to an individual, without the need for the physical healer, but not always. The aura of the healer often acts as a transformer, and sometimes this is necessary. For at source the transmitted energies can be too powerful for the recipient to receive on one occasion. Many factors will determine whether or not a recipient benefits from spiritual healing. Diet and general bodily maintenance naturally play a part, but trying to eliminate any underlying cause of suffering is also important.

Distant Healing

Distant healing can flow any distance in response to healing prayers. The healer does not require the presence of the recipient; indeed it matters not if they are on opposite sides of the globe. In its simplicity and potential effectiveness, it is similar to contact healing.

The power of thought, healing prayer effectively being an altruistic positive thought, is more powerful than most people realise. When anyone through prayer sends out a request for healing, particularly an accomplished healer, the thought acts as a carrier wave. Spirit helpers often assist this, effectively boosting the vibrational signal. They do so in order to ensure it reaches its intended recipient. The thought signal then acts in the same way as the aura of the healer through which it has passed, as transformer of healing energies.

In some cases distant healing is less effective than contact healing. It would be my guess to suggest that some people need the reassurance of personal contact, and the counselling of human one-to-one togetherness, whether professional or simply a good listener. While it is equally true to say that some people respond better to absent healing. Particularly those who with contact healing might put up a mental barrier and by the negative (repelling) vibration they instil within their aura, neutralise the positive effect that the healing energies can have. But, when distant healing is transmitted, and on a conscious level they are unaware, they do not repel the positive waves of energy.

Psychic Surgery

At times what is termed "psychic surgery" can be similar to and even utilise spiritual healing, with healing energies being transferred to a recipient. However, it can also go further, and involve surgical procedures. These are generally performed while the healer is in a state of trance, when a spirit healer or doctor, as with general trance mediumship, utilises the physical faculties of the medium.

More often than not no obvious physical instruments are used, although the controlling spirit seems capable of handling spirit equivalents which remain physically invisible. Treatments can involve the opening and closing of wounds, although the only physical evidence, which might remain, is occasional small marks, and these generally fade within a day or two.

Procedures beyond the abilities of current earthly capabilities have been recorded. However, like all forms of healing, no healer or psychic surgeon can guarantee 100% success.

All mediums are wonderful to witness or experience, especially those more accomplished. Unfortunately, as in many walks of life, rogues who seek financial gain also exist. But with an open-minded approach, via reputable established organisations such as the Spiritualists' National Union, or one of the many independently run groups, genuine mediumship is available for all to witness and enjoy. For there is little more uplifting than to personally receive conclusive proof that life truly is eternal.

CHAPTER 5

HOW THE SPIRIT LINKS
WITH THE PHYSICAL BODY

As can be gathered, by information already given concerning the aura, while upon earth we are, what would seem to us, a complicated mixture of structured energies. Initially, pre-birth, they form what is probably best described as a 'matrix'. Around this the physical body is constructed. As each part of the 'matrix' resonates at its own predetermined frequency, this draws to it tiny sub-atomic particles of matter which themselves resonate at sympathetic frequencies; these, in time, join together to form the structure and matter (bone and tissue) of the physical body.

In total, while upon earth it is generally accepted that we are sevenfold spiritual beings. Although upon higher levels of existence this might 'extend' to a number more. We largely do not remember our divine heritage, and the glorious future that is forever ours, a future that will span throughout aeons of time, for all eternity. If we could but truly know ourselves, in all our glory, we would realise our power, which extends to and, beyond, the imagination of humankind.

I believe it is useful to understand how the spirit links with the physical body, and this knowledge I, to my own degree of understanding, will endeavour to explain. Not in scientific terms, and perhaps not in the terms which might one day be used and hopefully fully understood by all; but my explanation is, I trust, simple and straightforward to understand. Basically, it can be said that the spirit links with the physical body through our finer energy bodies and that these contain chakras, which are energy centres or vortices. These connect through to corresponding glands; and from these along meridian pathways to organs, then onward to nerves, blood, bone, tissue and all parts of the physical body, with not a cell excluded from vibrational connection.

The finer energy bodies could be likened to fields or envelopes of energy, or indeed to levels of consciousness, which encircle and interpenetrate the physical body via the chakras; the word chakra being of Sanskrit origin, and signifies a 'wheel'. I believe that each of the finer energy bodies and chakras have their own frequency range, which intertwine with the adjoining frequencies. When seen clairvoyantly or through aura photographic techniques, which I do not believe reveal the full extent of the finer energy bodies, they produce an appearance of ever shifting and changing mixtures of coloured patterns. Each finer energy body and chakra having a balance or mid-point to its range, an ideal or optimum frequency, at which rate, if we are in perfect harmony, they will vibrate more distinctly. When, because of some inharmonious thought or action, or because of some external interference, they 'stray' from their ideal frequency, mental, emotional, or physical stability or health can be affected.

The finer energy bodies can also be considered as transformers, in the sense that they are each capable of receiving and recording vibrational 'messages' or 'signals', and where appropriate relaying or transmitting the information. They process all forms of information, thoughts, feelings, impressions, and actions at all levels, physical, emotional, mental and spiritual. They are in effect receiving, transforming and sending 'stations' of immense sophistication, capable of evaluating every scrap of information received. None of this is done on what we might consider a conscious level. It is effectively an automatic and super-efficient natural function of the finer energy bodies, carried out at an unconscious level via the chakras, which have counterparts in each of the finer energy bodies, and can be considered as energy centre linking points.

The finer energy bodies are composed of increasing, or progressively finer or subtler forms of ethereal (or sub-atomic) matter, as they extend outwards. It might be concluded therefore that we are *energy beings*, temporarily connected and functioning through a physical body, which itself is a form of energy.

Each of the first four bodies has natural potentials for higher or lower aspirations, which confront us with the need to experience lessons. If these are successfully undertaken they help to transform us for the better, and the rate of vibration of our finer energy bodies becomes higher, thus our lessons are like stepping stones that assist our spiritual growth.

In the following list, numbers 1 to 4 relate more to the personality or the lower self, while numbers 5 to 7 relate to the higher self. I have chosen to use what I consider the most appropriate names to describe the finer energy bodies although, in some teachings, a number of other names are at times used.

Number 1. Elemental. The elemental body is the closest to the physical body, which also has its own electromagnetic counterpart. It is linked with the base chakra, located at the base of the spine. It is said to link with the adrenal glands, and along the meridian pathways with the kidneys, colon, spinal column, bones and legs.

It is the grounding body that draws or connects us to earth, as a cohesive bonding link it enables the spirit to bind to the physical, while it also attempts to balance our earthly elements. To maintain a healthy state at this level of being it is every person's responsibility to care for his or her own physical body.

To where possible, have an adequate and healthy diet, and to take a reasonable amount of exercise. If we are over active we become tired, because we are pushing the body too hard. While if we are under active we become lethargic, because the body is insufficiently used.

It is said that each of the bodies has what might be termed an optimum period for growth and development; and for the elemental and physical this term is during the first seven years of life. If any health problems are insurmountable during this seven-year period, the resultant weakness could remain for life. While on the plus side, it is during this period that the physical form repairs more easily.

As can be gathered, and I am sure appreciated, a healthy balance is not necessarily easy to achieve or maintain; rest and activity in moderation are required, along with harmony in all actions. If this level of the aura is seen clairvoyantly, in a healthy condition, it will appear predominantly clear bright blood red.

Number 2. Vital. The vital body is linked with the spleen chakra, located in the proximity of the spleen near the navel. It is said to link with the gonad glands, and along the meridian pathways with the womb, ovaries, testicles, genitals, bladder, spleen, and nervous system.

This body is the container of the vital energy received physically from the sun, and superphysically from the ever-flowing spiritual reservoirs of life-force energy. It is called the vital body because it is the one that gives vitality to the physical.

The vital body, like the physical and all our bodies, expands and develops, although in the case of the finer energy bodies the expansion is of consciousness or awareness (spiritual progression), and not to be confused with physical growth. Its optimum period for development is said to be between the ages of 7-14 years; when it is best equipped to learn from its dual potential of lower and higher aspirations, although its understanding and development can continue throughout a lifetime.

The natural potential of the vital body may sound disturbing; it is towards fear, hate, anger and violence. But there is a reason; it is because at the 'animal' level of our being all of these can be necessary for survival. Our aim is to learn our lessons so that we can master these feelings, and transform them into feelings of love, compassion, fearlessness and friendliness, along with understanding.

The vital body oversees every atom and cell of the physical body, and recognises every imbalance and deficiency, and attempts to keep the balance correct. If necessary, because a deficiency is insurmountable, it will choose to keep one aspect going, such as a vital organ, to the detriment of other aspects. Breakdowns in health are unavoidable when vital energy sustaining substances are too depleted. If seen clairvoyantly, in a healthy condition, it will appear predominantly clear bright orange.

Number 3. Astral. The astral body is linked with the solar plexus chakra, located at the base of the sternum. It is said to link with the pancreas gland, and along the meridian pathways with the stomach, liver, gallbladder, pancreas and nervous system.

This is the body of desire, often called the emotional body. If desire is too strong this body will appear coarser with colours less than beautiful. When we recognise the reality of spiritual life and our purpose for incarnation, and align this with our emotional desires and reactions, the astral body grows finer with colours more beautiful. Although these can change rapidly, as emotional changes occur. It is said that the astral body generally has its optimum period for growth between the ages of 14-21 years, or puberty to adulthood, when we are confronted with the need to learn so much concerning emotions. This body very easily influences any or all thoughts. It absorbs feelings of love, of caring, along with the opposite, of hate, as well as fear, experiencing and expressing through the physical sensations of touch, sight, speech and hearing. It has the potential for doubt, for emotions can cloud the thinking, but once we learn to understand our emotions we can develop trust and awareness, and gain clarity in our thinking.

At the onset of a shock or trauma the ethereal structure of the astral body shrinks, as does the solar plexus chakra, causing the glands and organs it links through to likewise shrink, or to become restricted. If this is very severe it can block the flow of energy along the meridian pathways, and cause physical damage, as the tissue is constricted and cannot move or function properly.

Under such circumstances, those with the ability to see the aura would see a smaller or contracted aura, as well as one with murkier or darker colours. To keep the astral body in balance it needs calmness and tranquillity, allowing it to perceive clearly.

If seen in a healthy condition, the astral body appears predominantly as a glowing yellow, and when reaching towards the next level of consciousness, would take on a brilliant golden yellow, indicating clarity in the emotions.

Number 4. Etheric. (Or, Lower Mind). The etheric body is linked with the heart chakra, located over the heart. It is said to link with the thymus gland, the immune system, and along the meridian pathways with the heart, lungs, circulatory system, arms and hands.

This is the body of formal mind, and is an instrument of more concrete (down to earth) thought. It should be more dominant than the astral body; to be the controlling body of earth-will although, sometimes, the astral body of desire can reverse this role, causing one to become extremely sensitive, highly volatile, easily upset, irrational and undisciplined.

The etheric body is responsive to all that is happening throughout the other lower and subservient bodies and, provided the astral is not allowed dominance, will direct operations, stimulating conscious thought with creative ideas and awareness, which is part of its function. It is also the memory body for the lower bodies and itself, and the pivot, or linking body to the higher bodies and consciousness. To keep it in balance, it needs reason to be brought to bear, and calm thinking, which will also help the other bodies. The effect of stress, worry or fear can cause this body and the heart chakra to shrink, and the flow of energy along the meridian pathways to become restricted or blocked, causing physical constriction first to the thymus gland, then to the heart and lungs. The optimum period for the growth of this body is said to be between 21-28 years of age.

The etheric body embraces imagination and dreams. While if this is transformed towards higher aspirations, it can develop the potential for clairvoyance, and greater determination and will. If the etheric body is seen in a healthy condition, it appears predominantly bright green, and when it is seen as bright emerald green, this indicates stability and power.

Number 5. Mental. (Or, Higher Mind). The mental body is linked with the throat chakra, located over the throat. It is said to link with the thyroid gland, and along the meridian pathways with the lungs, throat and mouth.

This body is at the level of abstract mind, free from the self-imposed restrictions of the ego. It absorbs and stores the knowledge we gain from the myriad of experiences and lessons of our lower bodies. It is located beyond, or around, and interpenetrating with the etheric body. In the course of evolution, we need to develop so that the mental gains domination over the etheric, astral and other lower bodies. Then we can free ourselves from the ego, and eventually the circle of rebirth.

The directional influence of the mental descends into the etheric level of consciousness through the intuition or conscience, giving inspiration, discipline, planning, humility, will with power, love and balance. When seen the colour of the mental body appears predominantly azure (sky) blue,

Number 6. Spiritual. The spiritual body is linked with the brow chakra, located over the forehead. It is said to link with the pituitary gland, and along the meridian pathways with the left eye, ears, nose, the nervous system and the lower part of the brain.

This is the body or level of consciousness of spirit intellect and intuitiveness, of true spiritual knowledge, truth and wisdom. Of insight and enlightenment, where personality no longer dominates. Instead, a greater oneness with all life is understood, with a greater perception of reality, of being. The level of consciousness to which it is believed the Buddha, and many others throughout history, had reached, and in consequence were considered divine messengers of God. The spiritual body, if it is seen, appears predominantly indigo (dark blue).

Number 7. Celestial. The celestial body is linked with the crown chakra, located over the crown of the head. It is said to link with the pineal gland, and along the meridian pathways with the right eye, the higher part of the brain, and the nervous system.

This body is by many, particularly in Indian teachings, said to be the body of 'ultimate' (to our present understanding) spiritual attainment, and while I describe it as a body, it is also said to be a bodiless level of pure spirit consciousness. Having the ability to access and merge with levels of higher thought, and thus form a link with all previous knowledge and with still higher levels of consciousness. From this level we can, if we so wish, move-on to expand our awareness on pathways at present undreamed of, and perhaps currently beyond our comprehension. The celestial body, if glimpsed, appears predominantly violet to purple.

These are the bodies, or levels of consciousness, which are in greater use whilst we are in physical form. Although, it is probable that there are still higher bodies, if they can still be called such. For it is a certainty that higher levels of consciousness exist into infinity. With these higher levels of consciousness only awakening, so to speak, when our level of attainment reaches certain awareness, and until then they lay almost dormant.

In addition to being the finer energy bodies' link to the physical body, the chakras and meridians are centres and pathways for the flow of life-force energy. The base chakra draws strength from the earth's energies to give us basic physical strength, while the other chakras draw more refined and progressively higher vibrational spiritual or superphysical energy from the atmosphere. This energy is vital to our well being, it flows into and stimulates the physical body via the glands, and it is when the flow of this life-force energy is restricted that we are more likely to become ill.

When the chakras are in a healthy condition they have (clairvoyantly) been seen to spin or pulsate at great speed, the base chakra being the slowest, and they become progressively faster upwards to the crown. When the chakras spin at their healthy rate we are healthy and full of life and vigour, when they slow down disease can set in, and if they all stop it is the conclusion or end of our current physical life. But the spirit continues its journey, forever seeking, learning, developing and expressing itself according to its level of consciousness. (Yes, you too, really are a remarkable being).

CHAPTER 6

THE SPIRITUAL LAW OF CAUSE & EFFECT
FREEWILL AND SUFFERING

Cause and effect is a spiritual law that affects us all, regardless of whether we have understanding of it, or whether we are in spirit or upon earth. What we think, say and do, are causes, the resulting consequences are effects. Naturally, there are good and bad consequences, according to the causes we initiate.

The effects produced by the many causes we instigate during our lifetime can sometimes be immediate. For example, if you hold your hand in an open fire the effect will be to very quickly burn yourself. Or, the effect can be far-reaching and might manifest at a later stage of this lifetime, in spirit, or in a future physical lifetime. For the many causes we invariably initiate can be of a straightforward nature (as the fire burning) or of a very complicated nature. Life, in a way, is one long cause interspersed with a series of effects. Regardless of whether we have started to experience the effects upon earth, we will upon our passing. For the realm we find ourselves within will itself be one indication of the lifetime we have lived. All will be in accordance with the outworking of the natural law; or we could say natural justice, for the consequences will be in accordance with absolute and perfect justice, which seeks to educate not punish the soul. Although in many ways we may punish ourselves. For a soul who upon passing finds him or herself in a lower and thoroughly unpleasant realm may, because of the guilt and shame they feel, prolong their personal anguish.

What it is important to know and remember is that the law of cause and effect is at all times in operation. There are no exemptions and no escape. You cannot dodge it, and it does not come into play with only the major things in life. Every little cause produces an equally measured effect. I say this not to frighten anyone, but because it is fact. The average person has nothing particular to fear, for let us not forget that all the seemingly minor causes of a good nature will effect in what we would consider a favourable way. We should remain vigilant though. For our futures will be more pleasing if we can eliminate also those little negatives, such as those of the ego. The ultimate choice in everything we think, say, or do, is always our own. For we have and always will have freewill, which is our right to choose. We can be kind and loving at one end of the scale. While at the other, cruel, hateful or evil. How we use our freewill, whether wisely or poorly, it is nonetheless subject to the law of cause and effect.

Generally speaking, if we are using our freewill wisely we will be following a loving, caring and sharing pathway. Theoretically it should be simple to do so, for our inner knowing of the heart, our conscience, and our inner sensing, our intuition, will, if we follow their guidance, advise us well. But, and again, we always need to be vigilant, for that ego aspect of self can run amok, and the temptations of an over indulgent physical world have led many to turn their backs upon the spiritual and ignore inner guidance.

Freewill, is a birthright given to us by The Power, the source of our very existence. If anyone attempts to usurp this in any unjust way, it is a spiritual violation that, by the outworking of the law, they will be held accountable to the appropriate degree to match their misdeed. If we can avoid all of life's pitfalls, and I am sure we can all think of many, then we will be moving towards becoming finer spiritual beings, and furthering our spiritual progression, rather than creating undesirable repercussions.

It is important that we should all be aware that spiritual progression is not simply tied to those aspects of life considered major. But that every single thought, word and deed in life is, to appropriate degree also important. For, so often it is the "little things" that go to make so much of life. If we can be polite, friendly and above all honest to our higher spiritual aspirations and in all of our dealings with others, without ulterior motive, and without unduly judging others, for we do not know the pathway they have trod, then we will indeed be living justly, and creating a fine spiritual future for ourselves. It is inevitable, because cause and effect is the supreme law of life.

When we understand this law, it becomes clear that it is when it is impinged that the consequences often materialise as suffering, and this can be mental, emotional, or physical, for it disturbs our equilibrium, or balance. The outworking of cause and effect can also bring other consequences, which are equally inevitable. One who gives only a little love will receive little love in return; one who hurts others will feel hurt in return, and so forth. In time all our thoughts, words and deeds will bring effects of equal measure, for cause and effect bring balance. It is in effect a cosmic teaching aid.

If someone is unkind, greedy, selfish, rude and uncaring, deluding themselves with untruths, lying to others, expressing no compassion, friendship or love, they will reap accordingly, and suffer the consequences. These, as mentioned, can manifest in the physical, as bodily ill health or disease. This is because at a deeper level of being (not necessarily a conscious level) some aspect of self knows when we are behaving in a manner unbecoming of an eternal spirit being, and this quite naturally can have an adverse effect upon our actual bodily cells.

We do tend to think of the spirit and the physical body as being two separate bodies or states of being, whereas the reality is that all life, and all the bodies we possess, are composed of spirit matter or energy. Therefore when what we might for simplicity call negative energy lodges within one body, it will inevitably have some influence upon all other bodies. When we behave in a negative (disharmonious) way this can hinder and in extreme cases cut us off from the natural flow of divine energy. By so doing we can weaken our protective energy, disturb our finer energy bodies, and allow disease to manifest at the cellular physical level of being.

Negative energy, or a discordant vibration, can enter the physical body through one or more of the chakras. Which one (or ones) being dependent upon the nature of the 'disturbance', from where it travels to the nearby physical gland(s) and reverberates along the meridian pathways. Where subsequently, if prolonged or severe, it effects the vibration and function of the organs. Once this occurs the problem is more noticeably reflected in the health of the physical body. But, if we restore harmony to our finer energy bodies and chakras, the glands and organs will 'receive' what amounts to a healthy vibration. Once this happens, if the problem has not progressed beyond recovery, they will automatically begin to return to health. This is why spiritual healing can be most effective, for it seeks first to bring harmony to the spirit through the aura.

If we look deep within and listen to our conscience and intuition, then we will generally find ourselves capable of finding why we are suffering, and we can then take action to remedy the cause, not simply treat the symptoms.

We tend to think of each lifetime as singular and separate from the previous. Yet through the law of cause and effect we learn that what we think, say and do in one lifetime, can and will influence us at some time in our future, possibly in our very next lifetime. Therefore, while in one way we quite rightly consider each lifetime in a singular way, and each is a singularly unique personality experience, it is in reality only another expression, for experience, in the one eternal, continuous and never ending spirit life.

Mental stress, fear and guilt in particular are modern-day causes of suffering. For the disharmony they generate within can quite easily manifest through to the physical aspect of being. To clear these causes they must first be identified. Then a process of evaluation, reduction and elimination can begin. Although not necessarily easy, it most certainly is possible to put this process into practise. Much will depend upon individual circumstances and, where necessary, the ability of the individual concerned to change casual circumstances. This naturally requires an appropriate degree of willpower and desire.

My personal understanding is that if you are suffering but do not know why, you should delve deep inside and really feel, with heart, soul, and intuition, for the reason. Looking far deeper than the programmed face values of the ego. During this exploration into your true emotions, it is the true root cause of the problem you must reveal. This may sound obvious, but it is surprising just how many people are continually living with false outward values, which are not representative of how they truly feel within. They are living by values which they 'believe' are expected of them by family, friends, neighbours, work colleagues, and society in general.

We have all too often been programmed to accept the 'system' which can pull against the direction of the spirit, causing body tension and tightened muscles which restrict circulation, and which can later contribute to a number of physical health problems. Once the root cause has been identified, self-help can be applied to eliminate its influence upon the mind. Self-critical evaluation of your emotions, thoughts, words and deeds may be necessary to really analyse and feel what makes you as you are. Positive thinking must play its part, when you find fault with yourself, for none of us is perfect or blameless. You must not say, "that's me, I can't change" because this is not true - *we can all change*. The first step is identifying your shortcomings, and then having the wisdom and honesty to admit them to yourself, not necessarily to others, unless apologies are required; then the self-work, the reprogramming, can begin.

Finally, it is important that we acknowledge our own self-worth. For if we do not care for ourselves on a conscious level, we might be sending a signal to the subconscious mind, which controls a great many bodily functions, unintentionally telling it not to bother caring for us on a physical level.

If you do need help the following seven-point 'check list' is a guide to show what might be considered, and perhaps need to change.

1. Always consider your true heritage, as an eternal spiritual being. You have read how important it is to live in harmony with the natural laws; are your thoughts, words and deeds worthy of an eternal spiritual being? If not, *you* have the power to change them.

2. Be true to yourself and what you know is right, know yourself, be yourself. Do not live by the values and expectations of others, live by your own true feelings; use your inner instinct and intuition. Take charge of your destiny, take personal responsibility, and do not allow others to dominate your decisions, to take *your* power. Ignore the stereotype images or ideals projected via the advertising media, newspapers, magazines, TV and such like. They are a form of 'brainwashing' designed to control your thinking, your attitudes, your behav-

iour, it is not just your money they are after, it is your mind, for once they have that they have everything.

3. If in conflict, especially in partnerships, be prepared to compromise on occasions, but not always, fifty-fifty is ideal. Consider all the positive aspects in all relationships, whether sexual, social, or working, and do not dwell on the negative, if there are more pluses than minuses then you should be reasonably contented. Sometimes it is a good idea to consider the hardship many people in the world endure, to appreciate fully how fortunate most of us are. (A man with no shoes thought himself deprived, until he saw a man with no legs).

4. Do not be afraid to ask for help, we all need it at times, remember we are all upon earth to learn, and our main teachers are each other. Never 'bottle' things up, seek healing, Spiritual healing or whichever you feel will benefit you at the time. Ideally, combine this with some form of self-help or self-healing.

5. If change is necessary, without overdue haste, draw-up a sensible well considered plan. Then, when you feel the time is right, follow it through. Try to consider all eventualities and consequences, so you know it is truly what you want, and that it will lead to 'betterment', but be careful, this must not be pure fantasy. The betterment you seek may not be financial, but if it gives greater happiness, peace of mind and contentment, this will relieve stress and be of benefit currently and for your future health. (It is worth knowing that life-changing decisions can sometimes give the body the impetus to heal itself of even the most life threatening of diseases).

6. Put self first, whenever appropriate, without deliberately seeking to hurt others, naturally, without opting-out of responsibilities and important commitments. If others feel threatened or confused, or in some way put out by your change then this is regrettable, but is unavoidable, for you cannot live to please

others to the detriment of self; for this is not being honest to yourself. Additionally, if you are not being honest to yourself, you will be denying yourself expression, and your freedom to give and receive love will be limited, for your spirit will be stifled. Indeed how can you truly hope to give and express unconditional love to others, if you do not love yourself enough to free your own spirit?

7. Be positive, be brave, and be different if it is right for you, no matter if others disapprove, because you are not living by their values. The current values upon this planet leave much to be desired, and without doubt need to change, for it is the established 'normal' behaviour that is polluting and destroying the planet. Which has left millions to die of starvation while farmers are paid not to produce an abundance of crops, because it would lower the market price, and these are just a couple of examples of 'normal' people, so who wants to be 'normal'?

I hope my "doctor Jim" efforts prove useful to those in need. They represent what I have learned and believe. Although I freely admit that things are not always easy to put into practise, and I speak from personal experience, it is important to realise that by spiritual law we truly are at all times in charge of self, and that ultimately we control our own destiny. We just need to locate the inner strength we all possess. (Keep digging, it's in there somewhere).

CHAPTER 7

EARTH IS A SCHOOL,
REINCARNATION ANOTHER TERM

Life is a spiritual learning experience. There is no such thing as death. Nobody, in the entire history of human existence has ever truly died! This is a fact. The physical body perishes, but the spirit essence that each of us is, is eternal and indestructible. So after the passing we call death, we continue to live, and we do so as the individual conscious spirit being we are. Capable of decision making, conversation, communication, with a spirit body that possesses fully intact sight, hearing and limbs, for we are rejuvenated as the perfect eternal being we, in essence, have always been.

It is estimated that the planet earth was created some three or four thousand million years ago, but regardless of whether or not this estimate is accurate, it is without doubt that earth was created for a purpose. Spiritual teachers throughout recorded history have told us that there is an order to the universe. That nothing happens purely by chance. That behind *all* there is purpose, and a plan. There may well have been a 'big bang' as the scientists call it. But that even this would have been by design, by natural law, and not an accident, or some cosmic fluke of nature that just so happened to spawn the creation of mother earth and eventually lead to the development of the human race.

Earth (and no doubt other planets too) was created for spirit evolution, and as a school for spiritual development and progression. One where, amongst myriad lessons and experiences involving countless situations and relationships, we must seek to evolve and develop into finer spirit beings (to in a sense master ourselves). As individual spirit beings we have freewill, although this does not give us the right to do as we please without accountability. For our freewill does carry responsibility, so it is not without repercussions and consequences. To develop as finer spirit beings we have to learn to use our freewill wisely, without harm to self, others, or the planet and its environment.

On a cosmic scale, we could be likened to individualised cells, or units, existing within The Great Spirit -- a fittingly descriptive name given by our Native American friends for The Power, The Source, God, or All That Is, to quote other titles or expressions used. Each individual cell is capable of changing form to suit its environment, but always carrying within a spiritual yearning, a desire, to experience the attunement and oneness, the perfect love, of creation. Even though we are linked to this perfect love at all times, to realise so in the fullest measure, we have a multitude of experiences, and stages of progression yet to experience.

Our preparation, the 'test', is for us to 'earn' the right of progression, which is 'measured' and expressed through our spiritual evolutionary growth. For each stage and level of progression we reach along our eternal journey is naturally absorbed within our essence. So there is no short cut, we cannot progress to a higher state of being by desire, we have to earn each reward along the way by developing and growing through our experiences, by our own efforts. The common 'error' of humanity, is for us to consider ourselves as entirely separate from each other and from nature, as totally individual and unaccountable beings, when in fact we, and all life, is connected; and what effects one, to greater or lesser degree, effects all.

We came to earth to learn through experiences, evolve, and

along the way to serve each other, it is time we understood, acknowledged and accepted our responsibility. To do so, we need to accept the truth of what we are, that is, spirit beings; and to realise, or effectuate, the abilities we each have and the deeper love we all possess.

On a higher level, when in the spirit life, our boundaries are more extensive, for we can travel the world and beyond by projection of our thoughts and spirit bodies and we can communicate with and learn from great teachers. While on our earthly level many of our limitations are created by our own fears, which are heightened by our failure to comprehend our true heritage as eternal spirit beings. If we were to truly understand our own abilities, we would find that we could mentally travel the universe. For even though we are in physical form we are nonetheless spirit beings, and if we could but release our spiritual minds, they would be free to explore far and wide.

It is time everyone in this world knew that they are eternal spirit beings; with responsibility and accountability. Denying this fact, as so many do, serves no purpose, for some day, sooner or later, all must face up to what they are. So many measure their successes in terms of physical comfort and security, but on a higher level of consciousness we measure ourselves by how much, through experiences, we have learned.

The physical form, which is necessary for us to incarnate through, does seemingly present us with a limitation of consciousness. But this too is a lesson, for we have to work to discover and understand ourselves. Our seeming physical limitations might appear to present us with more disadvantages than advantages but, when viewed objectively from a long-term spiritual perspective, our physical form can be better appreciated. For through it we learn at the deeper physical level of consciousness, and at the deeper emotional level. It is necessary for us to learn through personal experiences, since the physical experiences are of far greater significance than any conceptual understanding.

While in no other state is our freewill boundary so extended, affording us great scope to experience. But we need to take care, for on the potentially adverse side it does also make it more possible for us to transgress the boundaries of right; something we would not do when purely in spirit form. Intuition here, acts as our guide, our conscience, to what is right and wrong and fair and just. So, for better or for worse, while in physical form we can extend our freewill expression to reach new heights or sink to greater lows. But, as the previous chapter outlined, we are always fully responsible for all we do. For although we are free spirits, which allows us to do 'wrong', it is us in spiritual essence, by our level of consciousness, who judge our own right from wrong, so cause and effect in a sense is a self-teaching aid.

Unlike our earthly schools, which generally have a set-leaving timetable regardless of whether we take or pass exams, we have found the need to keep returning to the school for humanity. Endeavouring to reach the stage of growth when our spirit will, metaphorically speaking, have passed all the exams necessary for our elevation to a higher dimension of life. For there are no short cuts, no favourable marking, and we cannot escape and progress with a lower grade than necessary, either we pass or we will need to continue our lessons, perhaps upon earth, and perhaps elsewhere.

During each lifetime on earth, every problem we encounter can be considered a lesson, a challenge to be overcome, for in this way our spirit grows. Progress comes as we recognise and outgrow imperfections; although these can be of a very subtle nature, and by doing so we develop towards perfection, leaving behind greed and egotistical concerns. Indeed, our seemingly most difficult problems and painful experiences can be the best lessons for our development. For it is only through such experiences of the depths to which we can all sink, that we can more fully appreciate the heights to which we can aspire. If we were to look beyond this lifetime, to mentally time travel forward to the day following our passing, we might better appreciate and view the consequences that our actions of today are creating for our tomorrows. Indeed, this is a mental exercise that I would recommend all to try.

Death, although not something to be dwelt upon in any negative way, is certainly not something that should only be considered far over the rainbow, to be contemplated only when one grows older, for its inevitability is with us from the moment of birth. It may take an unknown number, and perhaps many years to arrive, but arrive it will; while without doubt death has a definite part to play in the evolution and progressive development of our eternal spiritual consciousness. Ideally we should have understanding of 'death' from an early age, for we can never be sure when our time, or that of a loved one, will come. For to learn what death is all about can take away much anxiety and worry. After all, we would never ignore another so certain and so important of an inevitability.

When the time comes for our spirit to return home after an incarnation upon earth, in the spirit world, it is celebrated as the completion of another hopefully fruitful expedition, the end of another term at the school for humanity. With the journey having been undertaken in order to gain highly valued experience for the eternal spirit. This too is how we upon earth should learn to view 'death', as the end of term or school, and an aspect of one eternal experience.

Incarnation offers many 'life-lessons' as they are often called. Of course, cause and effect I consider the most important spiritual law of which to have understanding. There are also spiritual (sometimes called universal) laws that govern action, attraction, compensation, correspondence, gender (which can change lifetime to lifetime), polarity, relativity, rhythm, vibration, the transmutation of energy, and the oneness of life. While the lessons embrace aspects of charity, compassion, courage, dedication, faith, forgiveness, generosity, honesty, kindness, patience, responsibility, self-love, and ultimately unconditional love, and most likely more.

All these lessons and aspects we experience in myriad different ways and circumstances throughout our lifetimes upon earth. As you might imagine, since there are so many different ways in which each can be experienced, to learn all that they can teach cannot very easily be achieved in one short visit to earth, not even if we all managed to live for 100 years.

Many people do not realise that they have lived many times before; that when we complete an incarnation, we return to our true home, the spirit world, or heaven, as more generally called. But once there we do not rest-in-peace for all eternity, we continue with life, with relationships, with work, with hobbies and with learning. All undertaken with love which, on that higher level of consciousness, can more naturally be expressed than during earthly life, when the ego, the personality and an inability to comprehend the true nature of life, makes each of us more fearful and spiritually inhibited, clouding our judgement.

We are told that our time in the spirit world is fulfilling in its own right, but, a time comes when we begin to realise that we need deeper understanding of the lessons available through the experiences of incarnation. Lessons that can, more easily, be grasped through a myriad of physical experiences. So by freewill choice we seek to undertake another incarnation. Our desire and reasons are taken into consideration by those further progressed, those who guide in these matters, and can better see when and where we might be born in order to find the circumstances suitable to learn the lessons we seek. The plans are made (and this quite often can involve a group of people who have incarnated together previously doing so again), and when the time is right, and all is in place, we start another incarnation. We enter as a baby, hoping, without any guarantee of success, to learn those lessons of which, on that higher level of consciousness before birth, we all too clearly realised that greater experience was desirable. Here, our problems once again begin!

It would be guesswork to estimate just how many of us actually fulfil and experience all or even a reasonable percentage of our plans. But, judging by the state of the world, I would suggest that the success figures, if we were to put things into these terms, are not too high. Indeed, at times, it seems as though the dunces of the universe inhabit the earth. For once here, so many deny their spiritual nature and ignore and suppress any intuitive notion that physical life is not the be all and end all of existence.

Why do we need to reincarnate to experience? Because, it is of far greater value to have actual, rather than conceptual, understanding. While it is quite obvious by the earlier shown list of experiences to undertake, there are far too many to fully encounter in one brief lifetime. Conceptually, we cannot be told how it feels to experience so many earthly emotions and aspects of love at the grosser physical level of being; we have to experience the emotions for ourselves. All the other life lessons are similar; in that understanding the concept on a higher thought level is not the same as learning them through personal physical experience. For when personally experienced the lessons are fully absorbed, they in a sense become part of us, and at a much deeper level of consciousness, in more profound totality. We have to learn at this grosser level because spiritual progression is a series of stepping-stones. We can never move-up without sufficiently mastering all experiences at each level below.

As we evolve, through a great number of physical incarnations, and also in numerous ways and dimensions in spirit, we slowly progress or, to put it slightly differently, our consciousness or awareness keeps on growing and expanding. We have the capacity to continually expand our consciousness and, at the very root of our spiritual desire we undoubtedly seek to reach a level we might consider akin to godliness. Such a dream, to be as and at one with The Great Spirit, is perhaps the ultimate dream, and the natural higher desire of every soul.

As I have said, life is a spiritual learning experience, and if we do not learn from our experiences in one lifetime, we will need to return until we do. So it might be that we got things wrong in our previous incarnation and have felt the need to return and try again in this. But more alarming to consider is the possibility that we might have got things wrong during numerous previous incarnations, and might be stuck repeating the same old mistakes incarnation after incarnation. This too is a good reason why, having seen that the world and we are in need of change, we respond in this lifetime, and not ignore our own shortcomings and leave the problems of the world to others. Otherwise we might be living a lifetime without worthwhile progression, and find ourselves needing to return.

The pathway we should aim to follow is the one we might envisage or feel our spirit, our high consciousness, directing us upon; rather than the one our material programming might have us pursue. For the *seemingly* better pathways, those that materially satisfy and give physical pleasure to us should not be our only concern, for they are temporal, and not part of our long term eternal future. Eventually, we must all learn to follow the inner light of the spirit, to move towards spiritual perfection, and to follow the guidance of higher aspirations. If we are honest with ourselves, with our true inner self, it *is* what we want anyway. For beings of love, from love, is what we in essence are. We all want to feel and experience more and more, greater and greater love. We also want to share this love, to embrace all aspects of creation with it. These feelings are within us all. They are part of the nature of our being. But physical clouding and fear inhibits us, and causes us to stifle our true nature. The number one ongoing lesson for us all, is to find the courage to open the inner gates of the heart, so that this power, for love is the supreme power of The Creator, can more readily be released. Indeed all lessons are aspects of the one supreme lesson of learning to release the love at the core of our being. (You know I'm right, you can feel it if you try. It's why people are inspired to write songs and lyrics that sing of "The Power of Love", "Love Changes Everything", "All You Need is Love", and many more).

CHAPTER 8

THE MYTH OF RELIGION

Even though I was loathe to do so, I feel that it is important to give organised religion a mention within these pages, for it has played an infamously major role in known human history. Personally, and most thankfully, I was never indoctrinated into believing in anything they preach. Although, I do most fervently object when members of modern day clergy tell people that spirit communications are wrong. For, just like the TV psychologists mentioned earlier, they have blinkered vision, and absolutely no expertise in the subject upon which they attempt to preach.

Religion, in its organised human-made form can be traced back to ancient fear, superstition and myth, as my book *Religion: Man's Insult to God* dealt with. Some might say that it encourages people to live a good and righteous life, and in some cases in modern times this may be true. Yet today, as in its murky past, it still distils and encourages fear. It says, "Mediums call-up devils that impersonate your relatives and friends, so have nothing to do with them". In other words, do not seek the truth yourselves; "have faith" (in what they choose to preach) only. Indeed they esteem "faith" as the highest virtue, while denying truth.

Many human formulated religions have tried to dominate, while at the same time falsely claiming that they alone could save you. Mafia-style protection rackets are all they are. These human-made religions are not the holders of any spiritual, celestial, or heavenly power or authority. Nor can they forgive or bestow any special rites of passage upon anyone. We will all reap according to the supreme law, cause and effect, or the law of heaven if you prefer.

It is sinful for any religion to claim they possess any kind of authority, power or control over your immortal soul and eternal destiny. You are of God, an aspect; you are part of the eternal power. They cannot control or take away your spiritual birthright. They do not speak for God; they seek to dominate for their own ends. Even if these days it is often the blind leading the blind; in other words those that have been indoctrinated with false beliefs, now indoctrinating others with the same fallacies.

Another sin of religion is to deny genuine spiritual truths. For as mentioned, they instil fear and attempt to dissuade people from personal investigation, with threats of damnation and of a mythical hell of fire and brimstone. The only true hell is of our own making; no religion has the authority to condemn anyone. They are unscrupulous usurpers of power. Historically, they have caused more wars than any other force that has or ever will tread this earth. Indeed, their structured madness even reaches into modern times, still causing wars and individual acts of zealous barbarism and butchery. This fact alone should be enough to convince any sane person that to follow any religion is madness. Religion has hindered the spread of genuine spiritual truths, held it back, historically for the benefit of those who elevated themselves to positions of power and control, posts that are now occupied by the modern day clergy.

In brief, religion developed as follows. Although when reading this, please do allow for the fact that I am condensing several thousand years into a handful of pages. So it does speed through.

Ancient people at one time worshipped nature. When good crops and weather prevailed it seemed that good gods were controlling, so the people assumed they were pleasing to the gods. But when life threatening storms, floods and such like came, bringing fear, it was considered that bad or unhappy gods were in control. Thunder was thought to be the angry voice of a god, and lightning the gods' tool of punishment. (Earthquakes and volcanic eruptions were a damn good telling off!). It was reasoned that if a god saw fit to punish, then someone or something must have been displeasing a god. So the people, through lack of understanding, developed the idea that gods, just like themselves, would like gifts, offerings and ultimately sacrifices made to them. Some cultures offered vegetation or animals, while others went as far as offering human sacrifices. This eventually led to ritual, ceremony and ultimately to religion.

At another point in history it was the sun that became the focal point and supreme god of worship to a great many cultures, and we know of this principally from the Egyptians. It gave the people light, warmth and comfort, and caused all of nature to spring forth into life and growth. So the sun was naturally considered a good god. Ancient people, as people today, undoubtedly loved a good story, but they were most superstitious, and had nothing like the knowledge and advantages of modern education. For them it was not beyond belief to be told that the sun 'lived' a daily and a seasonal life. That it died at the close of day and was reborn at dawn, and grew 'old' (weaker) in winter and was 'rejuvenated' (stronger) in spring.

A further stage in history saw the development of ancestral worship. It is without doubt that amongst ancient people and throughout history, there have always been those who have had mediumistic abilities. The natural mediums of the tribes were able to see and communicate with passed tribe members. When they were physical mediums, others too may have witnessed spirit appearances and direct voice communications. As such sightings or communications became more regular, as around any developed medium they would, some took the role of overseeing what naturally became sacred occasions. Thus the early priesthood developed.

Over time, the priesthood, undoubtedly under other titles originally, became an established and recognisable position in society. Unfortunately, as its prestige and power as 'go-betweens' grew, human weakness led some of the early priests to become corrupt, for they realised that by trickery and manipulation they could profit for themselves. So the blessings from the departed or the 'gods', for all who proved their survival of 'death' were considered gods, became embroiled as a religious act, one dealt with by priests. At this point in history genuine mediumship obviously did not suit the corrupt priesthood, as this would have denied them the positions of power and authority that they made so lucrative for themselves. So they set about destroying the genuine mediums, first by ridicule, then by infamously cruel and murderous means.

These different phases of belief, and no doubt many more diverse ones around the globe, did not give way one to another overnight, all was gradual. This no doubt helping to appease those who might have objected to change, for historically this has never come easy to people. To make things less confrontational the old ceremonial dates were always used, only with new names and reasons given. Perhaps the then 'old timers', secretly if necessary, still celebrated such occasions in their own way, but gradually, as generation followed generation, the new reason was accepted.

The last major stage in the development of modern religion came about when a human character story was invented to replace the story of nature, its death (harvest) and resurrection (spring). I doubt that anyone knows for sure which culture first told the fable of the 'saviour' or 'son of God', although the oldest recorded in modern history is Osiris, some 3700 years ago in Egypt. The old myths of the past were then re-written and draped around the 'saviour'. This fable Christianity applied to Jesus (who most assuredly was a medium and healer).

Some blinkered Christians may still think that their religion is unique but it is not, it is a clear copycat religion. Before Christianity jumped on this particular bandwagon at the council of Nicaea in 325 AD (approximately 300 years after the physical death of Jesus), there were at least 16 other religions that, in their teachings elevated one character to the position of 'saviour'. The Emperor Constantine, who first changed the state religion of the Roman Empire to Christianity, had little choice but to follow this same pathway. Before the change Mithraism was the state religion, and Mithra was considered to be the Son of God, born of a virgin etc., etc., etc., in other words, almost identical to the life story that Christians teach of Jesus. So to replace Mithraism the new 'saviour' had to be elevated to this godly status to satisfy the simple minded people of those times. The establishment could hardly hope to replace a 'saviour-god' with a man. Therefore Jesus *had* to be elevated to at least an equally revered status. The same ancient mythological stories that had been around for a couple of thousand years before the emergence of Christianity were used and here and there relabelled with new character names to fit the plot, and just as all their predecessors had done, with renamed ceremonies continuing at the same dates as the old.

Why was the Roman Empire so involved in religion? Well, in those days the people were far more superstitious and easily led. To control civil, criminal and religious law, and in some areas these were intertwined, gave them complete domination over the average person. The laws demanded religious attend-

68

ance, rituals, ceremonies, and most lucrative funding. A percentage of income is even today demanded by certain religions.

Religion could have served a useful purpose in true spiritual guidance. Yet under whichever label, once it sets itself above the people, in a position of dogmatic control, telling people what to think and how to behave, it transgresses from helpful to a hindrance upon society.

I have tried to be brief; all I hope is that I have expressed my understanding adequately. I believe that religion is the remnants of a bye-gone age of fear, superstition and mythology (or story telling), and has no part to play in the process of distilling genuine spiritual truths.

CHAPTER 9

GENUINE SPIRITUAL TRUTHS

After the last chapter, which was unavoidably rather scolding, I thought you might enjoy reading some of those genuine spiritual truths or, to repeat from the Foreword, what I *believe* to be truth. If it becomes your truth (or already *is* your truth), I will be delighted. So for this chapter I have unashamedly 'borrowed' fourteen answers from my first question and answer book *Golden Enlightenment*, although I have abbreviated and here and there amended them. They cover many of the basic questions that new seekers upon the spiritual pathway ask. So with apologies to those who might previously have read them, I felt that it was important to include them for the benefit of new seekers. Although, by what you have read so far, you may already have grasped much of this knowledge, I hope after reading this chapter you will agree that it is reassuring to have certain specifics clearly defined.

1. When I pass to the spirit world, will I be reunited with my loved ones?

When you pass into the spirit world you will not only be reunited with your loved ones, it is likely they will come to meet you. You are of course an infinite spirit here and now, even though you currently function through your physical body. Since you are spirit, you cannot be truly separated from your loved ones. It is most likely that you have met them on many occasions during the sleep state, when your spirit is able to leave your physical body. This is basically the same process as 'death', except that during 'out-of-body' sleep experiences an energy link is maintained with your physical body, keeping it alive, and allowing your spirit to return.

Your brain, being a physical organ, is unfortunately unable to remember much, if any, of your sleep state meetings. Sometimes a small fleeting recollection may register, and you might think of this as just a dream, but it is often the fragmented memories of actual experiences. Although these can become clouded as they intermingle with other data that is passing through your subconscious mind.

2. Do children grow-up in the spirit world?

All life continues after 'death', regardless of the age at the time of passing. So when a child or a baby of any age, even a miscarried or aborted child, passes from the physical, spiritual growth continues. In the spirit world there are places of rest, and of learning, along with all the care and attention that any individual could possibly need. So development, growth and happiness are assured for all children.

3. What happens to suicides?

Those who commit suicide will, whenever possible, be met and cared for in the same way in which all are helped. There is no damnation or eternal punishment awaiting them. Usually those meeting them will be relatives or friends who love and care for them. Otherwise it will be a guide or helper who will care for them. Either way they will be comforted and treated with sympathy, compassion and encouragement.

4. Do animals survive 'death'?

As I have said, *all* life continues after 'death'. So, if you have lost a pet with which you built a bond of love you will, upon your own passing, find that the pet has survived 'death'. In the meantime he or she will be cared for and looked after either by one of your friends or relatives who will have recognised your mutual love, or by one of the many in the spirit world who engage themselves in the task of caring for such animals.

5. If I have married twice, do I have to choose between former partners after my 'death'?

Life in the spirit world is rather different from life upon earth. In a sense there are still 'rules', things you can do and things you cannot do. But these 'rules' are the universal or natural laws, not man-made rules. They are the laws of The Great Spirit, in operation.

Upon earth, over the centuries, many ideas of how life should be organised, controlled and ruled have been instigated. All of these ideas are human-made. In many cases, including marriage, they have no bearing or consequence, in the spirit world. Earth contracts or vows, written or verbal, cease at passing.

Life in the spirit world is in harmonious accord with the natural laws of The Great Spirit. Love in the spirit world is a matter of natural attraction in its purest form. Upon earth, as I am sure you are aware, attraction can be of a more superficial nature.

If you have had two, three or many more marriage partners it would not be of importance to those that have progressed in the spirit world. You are free to be with whichever partner you choose, provided your attraction and desire is reciprocated. Or if you so choose, you do not have to be with either or any partner. For each is a free spirit with total freedom of choice.

6. Why was I born?

You, like everyone else, chose to be born in order to learn lessons, through experiences and in this way, progress as a more enlightened spiritual being. Each physical lifetime teaches you a little more, until finally you will reach the level where you no longer need to return to earth. Although, even at this stage of attainment, you might still choose to be reborn, in order to serve as a teacher, or a healer, for the guidance and benefit of others.

7. Does it matter how I live my life, since I will survive anyway?

How you live your life is of great importance, not only does it have an effect upon your present day-to-day circumstances but it can also influence future incarnations, as well as life in one of the many realms of the spirit world. Ideally, you should strive to live in harmony with the yearnings of your own spirit, while duly respecting others. To do so, I suggest you use your inner feelings from the heart, or your intuition, and allow these feelings to be your guide.

You should recognise that the universal law of cause and effect, is forever in operation; guaranteeing, "As you sow, so shall you reap." Which means that through the law whatever you do in this lifetime will have repercussions that by natural law will affect your future; perhaps during this lifetime or in a future incarnation.

8. Is there anything to be gained by the understanding of survival after 'death', and by the study of spiritual teachings?

By understanding the factual truth of survival after 'death', and the knowledge that spiritual teachings bring of eternal life and natural laws, you should feel more encouraged to question every action of your life; thus potentially enhancing your spiritual growth and progression. As you judge yourself and your motives in all you say and do, with the realisation that you cannot escape the consequences of your thoughts, words and deeds, you have the opportunity to, and therefore should, become a more spiritually enlightened being.

Thus understanding should allow you the chance to make great advances in your spiritual progression.

9. Will I be judged upon 'death', and if so by whom?

Upon your 'death' *you* will be your only judge; although natural law will determine the level to which you aspire. In the fullness of time, to assist your understanding and to degree evaluation, you will be shown what will effectively be a replay of your entire life. You will judge or assess, with feelings of happiness and delight accompanying good and more pleasing moments and no doubt with sadness when you review moments of regret.

You should therefore fear no great day of judgement, with entry into heaven or hell the reward or sentence. At the same time you should consider that as your own judge you are likely to be very critical, and the ego cannot hide the truth. Others will not judge you, but your very vibrations will indicate your level of attainment and therefore, by natural law, determine the realm to which you will gravitate.

10. If the Great Spirit is all seeing and all knowing why is so much suffering permitted in the world?

The omnipresent consciousness - *The Great Spirit*, does not limit your spiritual growth by decreeing which lessons are available to you, allowing you the pleasure of one, while shielding you from another because it is painful. If this was so you would not develop with a complete or balanced understanding, and your spiritual progression and attainment would be restricted. The Great Spirit has given you freewill, and personal responsibility for all of your thoughts, words and deeds, and this gives you the choice of how, when and where you undertake to experience the many and varied lessons of life. Suffering might, on a higher level of consciousness and for specific reason be chosen, although it is more regularly the consequences of either your own past actions, or the collective freewill of others.

11. Why are some people born with physical or mental handicaps?

There could be several reasons why someone might be born into a physical body that is imperfect in some way. One possible reason, as mentioned in the previous answer, is that such a life was chosen on a higher level of consciousness before birth, so the individual spirit could experience and learn from the difficulties that such an incarnation might bring.

Not everyone can be neatly fitted into the category of "born to suffer" an experience predetermined before birth; accidents, mistakes and errors do occur, and it is humankind's freewill which is often to blame, for collective freewill can and does have an effect.

Therefore the many wrong actions undertaken by humankind during recent decades are producing effects that all too often cause innocent victims to suffer, for example, atmospheric pollution causing asthma. This is one of the reasons why it is so important for spiritual knowledge, particularly the law of cause and effect, to be understood by all.

12. Why do some people have an easier life than others?

Before birth you almost certainly have co-operated with more advanced spirit advisors to develop a life plan, in order to experience in what you have wished or needed to learn. The precision of this plan can be quite detailed and could have included knowledge of who your parents were going to be, the name you were to be called. Even the exact moment of your birth may have been calculated to attract certain astrological influences (vibrations). Most importantly, your plan is for certain personal experiences or lessons that pertain to your needs, to be undertaken for the benefit of your own (and possibly others) spiritual growth and progression. It is seldom desirable to incarnate into what we might, while using our physical senses, consider an idyllic life-style.

It might help if you think of yourself as an actor, one who has been cast to play the role most suitable for you at this particular stage of your acting career in a (very realistic) play titled "a life upon earth". Some may find a simple part playing an average person most ideal, while others are just right for the seemingly star role of hero or martyr. In this incarnation you play one role, and perhaps next time around you will play a completely different one. In the grand scheme of things, all will eventually balance fairly and you soon will have played all the parts necessary to complete a full and comprehensive program of learning; then perhaps you can take on the role of the director.

13. Why do some people fear spiritual communication and knowledge?

Ignorance is undoubtedly the reason for the fear many people hold for what they consider, "the unknown." They have some vague belief in life after 'death' but are opposed to spirit communication because they mistakenly believe this disturbs the so-called dead. They sometimes believe the 'dead' have gone to a place of rest, to wait a day of judgement and should not be disturbed until that day comes. They do not understand that the 'dead' cannot be disturbed, because they have never truly died.

When they communicate, directly or more commonly through mediums upon earth, spirits are not being 'disturbed' or 'called-up', they return because they wish to do so. Always it is the spirits who initiate communication, which is not possible without their desire to co-operate; for no medium can guarantee who will communicate. It is entirely the choice of those from the spirit world.

Many people who are afraid of the "unknown" would prefer it if the subject were never mentioned. What they perhaps unknowingly fear (and I say unknowingly because such a person rarely analyses why they are afraid) is the responsibility that spiritual knowledge and truth can bring. The discovery of spiritual truths does indeed bring responsibility. You can no longer blame fate or God for your good or bad fortune. Spiritual knowledge teaches you that every action and consequence of your life is your own personal responsibility. Indeed, through the law of cause and effect, it is possible that you are now reaping according to how you have sown in a past life. Understanding this law gives you the opportunity to take command of your life with a completely different, more positive and ultimately glorious outlook.

14. In the spirit world, do people there have bodies like ours?

People in the spirit world do continue to use a body; they use the soul body, which is as real and as tangible to them as your physical body is to you.

The only exception might be those that have progressed to higher realms. They have no need of the outward physical appearance to which you and I have grown accustomed. They still have a soul but this has been described as 'mist-like' if at all visible to those in realms below their own status.

However, for those spirit people who have not yet reached such levels of attainment, the body they use is a duplicate in appearance of the physical body they used when upon earth but without any defects. For example, if you had a physical body that was scarred, missing a limb, or with impaired vision when you passed into the spirit world, such defects would no longer exist. This is because physical defects do not affect your perfect soul body. Your soul body cannot become ill, nor can it be harmed. Furthermore, since spirit is eternal and ageless, if you pass in old age, it is most common to revert to an appearance from your prime. The way that you think of yourself will become your reality. If you pass over still young, you will mature only to an appearance you are happy with and not beyond. The perfect system you might say? And why not - it is heaven after all.

I hope you have enjoyed reading this chapter, if you would like to read more questions and answers, my book *Golden Enlightenment II* contains over 50 of them.

CHAPTER 10

ALL *IS* ONE, ALL *IS* GOD

It can rightly be said that "All is One" because there is only One, God (or Goodness omni-divided). Everything, every mineral, crystal, flower, plant, tree, insect, fish, bird, animal, and human, together with every star and planet (of which there are countless billions), the entire known and unknown universe, on all frequencies of vibration, exist within the multi dimensional One, and together make the 'body' of God.

To a degree all life can be measured by consciousness for as we progress our consciousness expands; we evolve and in a sense move 'closer' to God. As well as individual consciousness, there are many combined or interwoven groups, which form collective 'pools' of consciousness. These can involve just a few likeminded friends, to hundreds, thousands or even millions of people. These are the vibrations of those of similar or parallel thought or vibration. Like energy vibrations may combine to become collective pools of thought. There also exist collectives of such as national and world consciousness. If we go further, there is a solar consciousness and a universal consciousness. Within and pervading all this we have the ultimate and Supreme consciousness, (that which encompasses and through natural law directs All). This we might consider the mind of God, although this is not some far-off consciousness pulsating in some distant part of the cosmos, so no future star-ship will ever find it! Rather it is present, within and pervading all, for even the tiniest cell bears within the presence of mind. We can rightly consider that we are also aspects of the mind of God. That, the mind and 'body' of God is an energy matrix that encompasses and connects all of creation and all life.

Since we are not separate from the collective Whole, each of us can and do make a difference, an effect upon creation, even when we work to change the nature of our own thoughts and feelings. This will quite naturally be 'transmitted' to register within the collective Whole (sometimes called the collective unconscious). At the appropriate level of vibration, any personal change of consciousness is absorbed by The One and to degree made available to all humanity, for it becomes part of the universal mind energy to which we are all connected and are an aspect.

We are each from and of the Source: the Creator, and in essence have always existed. Each of us is naturally infused with the same energy as our Creator, although our ability to use or manipulate this energy is proportionate to our level of consciousness. We should never underestimate ourselves, for we are in essence pure, divine, and perfect beings. (I know it may be hard to believe).

Our purpose, the reason for our creation and existence, is twofold. On a personal level it is to expand our awareness through experiences, so that we might unfold or indeed awaken understanding of our perfection or divinity. At the same time our purpose is so that the knowledge and understanding that we gain can be absorbed and added to collective understanding. Although through many lifetimes we can acquire vast individual knowledge, indeed as some might term 'become seemingly great masters', we can never have the whole understanding of God - for the part cannot contain the whole. This may sound rather frustrating but on the positive side it does mean that there will always be more to experience and understand, so we will never become bored with our eternal existence.

Since we are all aspects of the Creative Source we should not be in competition with each other, for in a sense this puts us in competition with God. Instead, we should strive to be kind and considerate towards all people, all of creation, and towards ourselves. For no one is better than another or more of a divine spark. We are all equal and deserve to live with equal opportunity for growth.

'The One' has subjective as well as the objective aspects we see. In fact, the subjective aspects could be expressed in an infinite variety of ways in an infinite number of dimensions. It is clear, since all is really 'The One', that all of these yet to be recognised dimensions, including the spirit world, are interrelated, and interpenetrate with each other. (So all those 'alien' beings out there truly are your brothers and sisters, no matter what shape or form they presently take).

What many perceive as the emptiness of space, is not empty but is filled with energy elements that, under the natural law direction of 'The One', are capable of forming suns and planets. We can say with certainty that life did not develop by accident and was no cosmic fluke, rather it was effectuated by infinite mind, with infinite substance and that all is infinite within 'The One'.

Through the vast process of spiritual evolution we have progressed to individualised consciousness. One day we surely will progress to an expanded level of consciousness, to one that at our present stage of attainment would seem a level of super-consciousness. Yet even then, we will become aware of still vastly greater potentialities. The creative expression of 'The One' is part of us, and as our awareness grows, so shall we express our own understanding of that same creative power.

'The One', being *all*, gathers all experience, all learning, from all aspects and all dimensions of life throughout creation. Thus, 'The One' is at all times possessor of *all* knowledge. The Supreme Mind, the memory bank of 'The One', contains *all* knowledge, from *all* kingdoms of life: mineral, plant, fish, animal, human, angelic and many more life forms, on many planets and in many dimensions of existence. The Supreme Mind is the directive aspect of creation, within and part of *All*. Therefore, we are all directly linked with the Supreme Mind, directly with the mind of God; who works in and through every cell or unit.

Through this constant mind energy link, we too can gain access to the infinite knowledge of 'The One' (often referred to as looking at the Akashic records). However, we can only become aware according to our level of attainment; as we add one level of awareness to the next, another can be glimpsed and then slowly absorbed within our understanding. Then, as we extend our awareness, another level will open for us, thus gradually, through infinity, our level of consciousness will expand. We need only a minimal glimpse or thought of a higher level of awareness (a desire for greater knowledge) to begin the growth towards that level. This is how natural progression is made available, obtained, or brought forth.

Each person upon this planet is an individual spiritual being, an individualised aspect of God, with his or her own freewill and personal responsibility. Although, we commenced our spiritual growth, to spiritually evolve, at the humblest level of existence. Perhaps through aeons of time, we progressed to reach the human stage of individualised consciousness; we are told that individuality from this stage in spiritual evolution is maintained for all eternity. Nevertheless we will never reach the end of our progression. Over aeons of future time we will continue to develop, to infinity and we will always find experiences and ways in which to express.

We, as individuals within 'The One', have responsibility to each other, not to live life for others, not to shoulder their problems or carry them but by example and by whatever ways are practical, to help each other. If in no other way, then whenever possible, by revealing aspects of truth which we have been fortunate enough to discover. For truth (or an aspect of truth), is not ours alone to keep, for it really is time that all people had access to genuine spiritual truths.

On a personal level, we need to stand back and review our lives, to remove self from self, so that we do not let the ego obstruct our higher-self motives. We need to see things for what they actually are, rather than what, because of materialistic programming, we might have told ourselves they are. We also need to develop greater self-love; not loving ourselves to the detriment of others, but by behaving in a way that is befitting the spirit we truly are.

Where appropriate we also need to work on any of our own shortcomings, so that we can develop and project greater courage, charity, compassion, kindness and love. For in so doing, if we are genuine, we will advance such attributes upon this planet. Indeed, such attributes need to be advanced so that all people upon this planet can be relieved of the burden and torment of hunger and poverty. Thus, we can all live in peace and harmony, for how can any of us, while we continue to let such inequality exist, ever find true peace within?

It is time for individual people to take greater control. When enough of us desire change, and positively project and promote the thought that such change is coming, (or, better still is already with us, although yet to physically materialise), world leaders will be obliged to go along with the majority; indeed it will become their desire too.

We should never underestimate the value of our personal contribution, for we are spiritual beings, part of divinity, with power and choice, in fact we have much greater power than we realise. If we look within, with utmost honesty, we will find corners of the mind, of consciousness, where all the good imaginable is tucked away. We are in essence beings of love, but because of our programming this can be difficult to release. If we keep trying, keep chipping away, it will slowly emerge. (I haven't said it's easy).

Life is for sharing, not materialistic self-seeking; for we are *all* One; and to seek for self-only, denies 'The One', and denies the unity of *all* life. Sharing opens a two-way door, for as we give, so shall we receive. It is a spiritual law or truth and can be seen in operation in many ways. Kindness breeds kindness; compassion breeds compassion; love breeds love; but more than this, they can also transform or transmute, thus when love meets hate it does not repel, it embraces and changes it into love. All, of course, is subject to the manifest power within each of us, but even in the most stubborn of circumstances love will eventually (even if requiring many lifetimes) prevail. For it is the strongest, highest and purest form of divine power.

We truly do hold the key to change ourselves, and thus the world. Indeed, our inner world, our thinking, is of the greatest importance, for the whole of our external life is an expression or reflection of our personal and collective thinking. Therefore nothing in this world is beyond change.

As we change ourselves and thereby help deliver to the collective unconscious positive energies for change, these thoughts and feelings will become available to all who are in harmony (on a suitable vibration) via their subconscious link with this universal mind energy.

Everything upon this planet, life in all forms, is our collective responsibility. Collective responsibility begins with each individual; we cannot leave everything to others, for we are a part of the Whole. If we, collective humanity, want things to be better in this world, we have to make a collective effort but starting with ourselves and in this way empower the Whole.

We need to have pride in ourselves, pride in each other, pride in our neighbourhoods, pride in our nations and pride for the whole planet. This can only come about in its fullest sense when we are true to our higher aspirations, to others and to the whole of creation. When we can master this, we will find that we will also receive far more, for we will have spiritually matured and this will allow other energies, with still greater aspects and levels of goodness, to draw closer to us.

Within each of us is great power, for we truly are remarkable beings, of God and as God. If we fully understood ourselves we would find we could perform what would seem miracles, what restricts us and stops us are our own minds, through the limitations that our level of consciousness, through natural law, places upon us. Even in our seemingly restricted state, particularly collectively, we can make a vast difference to this world and, if we so wish, change it for the better.

My advice is to never limit your own potential or worth. Rather to keep working on your own self and when appropriate, offer guidance and assistance to others. For you, they and the world will reap just reward, even if in a future lifetime, so in eternity you will see the benefits. This may seem far-off but you are an eternal being, so the day will undoubtedly come.

CHAPTER 11

THE SPIRITUAL REALMS OF PROGRESSION

Astral (or etheric), mind, spiritual, and celestial, these are names given to those spirit world realms of which we have some knowledge. Although, our earthly knowledge of these realms is limited, particularly of the higher realms that in a sense have moved further away from physical concepts or understanding. The names themselves are not important and they do vary from teaching to teaching. What you may find useful to know is what they represent; and that is a progressive structure of levels of consciousness, which exist within the spirit dimensions.

The reason why different realms exist is because of the varying rates at which life, including us, for we are all in essence spirit, vibrate. We each vibrate at a rate that reflects our personal level of consciousness. The realms are representations of a variety of different levels of consciousness. With lower rates of vibration at the earth and darker realms levels and the highest rate touched upon herein at the celestial level. (Although the journey of the soul will eventually take us beyond the celestial level, which is the pinnacle level, of what is collectively called the spirit world).

The astral realm in many respects is said to be a replica of the earth plane. Therefore people find themselves within a realm similar to what, based upon their earthly experiences, they might expect to see. Although all upon passing are subject to the law of cause and effect, so if one has caused any adverse repercussions, these might adversely affect their immediate future existence. If so, they may then find themselves within one of the many undesirable lower and darker realms. Such realms being progressively dark and less desirable and more hellish the further one moves down the scale.

The lower realms have no doubt been "home" to many power hungry, greedy, selfish, cruel and evil people over the centuries. It is this type of person, by their own nature, who will be drawn to occupy such undesirable places. No doubt there are as many levels and sub-levels to such realms as befit the range of transgressions.

I say this not to frighten anyone but to educate, for our initial fate is in our own hands. Although, for those who do transgress, all is never lost. No one is ever condemned for eternity to a single realm, not even those considered the lowest or most evil. All life is progressive and just as we can progress in many ways upon earth, so we can progress in the spirit world. All is in natural increments, from one level or realm to another, one step at a time, as we open our awareness, find ways to serve and as we develop, slowly expand our consciousness.

The "first level" the average person may find him or herself upon, after their physical dissolution, is the astral, which as mentioned, is more a replica of the earth plane, only more accommodating. So if one fancies a drink, something to eat, or any other earthly type of pursuit or fancy, then most probably it will be open to them. Even though such things are no longer needed, for our spiritual bodies do not require physical sustenance.

Meetings with loved ones and old friends are most likely. Even if they now dwell at a higher level, for visiting realms or levels on a lower vibration is, by the natural lowering of their mind frequency, not only possible but a vital aid to progression. This allows those spirit people who are more progressed than ourselves to visit us upon earth, and thereby to assist the progression of those below them in the spirit world realms. Figuratively speaking the realms are like a chain, with those in realms above reaching down to form a link so that they can assist the progression of those in realms below. Thus it can be gathered that we are perhaps at all times instrumental to the progression of each other.

Service in the astral, as upon earth, can of course take many forms. It might be by returning to the earth plane atmosphere to help and encourage those who are earthbound, for some upon passing manage to ensnare themselves close to earth, sometimes because they are attached to someone or something, or because they are fearful or confused. Or it may be in helping those lower realm souls to move forward or make progress in some fashion. Or in assisting those more 'average' souls recently passed, whether they are adults, children or babies. It can be in furthering communication with those upon earth. Or passing to them encouragement, strength of mind, or inspiration in countless numbers of ways; to help or assist animals on earth, or those in spirit who perhaps await the passing of their earthly human companion, to name but a few more obvious examples. Or it can be in many, many other less obvious ways, such as artistic development and expression, since these too can be a form of service. For instance, a good comedian or artist in many forms of expression can bring upliftment to others. So service in spirit can be most pleasing and should not be confused with earthly duties or chores.

When one has progressed sufficiently, they next find themselves in the realm of mind. At the mind level of spirit life we find those who have progressed beyond the need for the earth-style pleasures, which a number in the lower parts of the astral still seek. Although, on all levels a sense of humour is most certainly retained and pleasurable leisure hobbies can still be enjoyed. But they have largely left behind the *need* to continue experiencing what they may at one time have loved when upon earth. Need and desire having been tempered by knowledge and wisdom, as the love of service in myriad ways of expression grows.

So we find that at mind level, by personal choice, service to those in the astral or upon earth may occupy part, in some cases much, of their time and thought. At this level there are groups dedicated to improving links with those upon earth in a continued attempt to provide evidence of survival, to give comfort through healing and to share spiritual philosophy. They seek to do so in the hope of awakening humanity to the greater truths of life, so that those of us upon earth might make greater strides in our own spiritual progression, rather than waiting until we get to the spirit world realms after our physical demise.

"Why bother, why not wait until your time comes?" so many ask. The answer is simple. It is because in the vast majority of cases people are not living in a way that aids their spiritual progression. They do not have caring, sharing and loving lives. They are living for themselves, busy in material and physical satisfaction, without any true concept of what is to follow. Effectively, they are living in ignorance of spirit and spiritual laws; in consequence many will find themselves in the lower realms.

I could ask those who believe ignorance to be bliss, a question. Do people not deserve to know the truth of eternal life and of spiritual laws and of the future they are without doubt sowing for themselves? The plain and simple answer is yes, they do. We should all know the truth of what awaits us over the rainbow. Such truths are not meant to be a mystery. Life is not intended as a mystery. It is a learning experience.

The Source of life does not ask you to guess the right pathway. The directional guidance is within spiritual mind and can, whether on earth or in spirit, manifest through conscience and intuition. Unfortunately, in many people these subtle levels of mind have been suppressed by indoctrinated religious and material thinking, and by physical desires and pleasures and media sensory bombardment. Of course not all physical pursuits and desires are bad but so many have been elevated to 'holy grail' status. We need to remember that all at this earth plane of being is temporal. Many people enjoy reading or watching TV mysteries. How many realise that there are still greater mysteries that lie within our own being? Where there are levels of mind that can be explored through meditation or quiet contemplation. Levels that will do more than delight your sensory perception, for they can also reveal your true self, your spiritual motivation, direction, feelings, inner wisdom, and bring a great sense of peace. In a sense it can open the gates of heaven to you. This is why sages tell us that the kingdom of heaven lies within. Your true inner self or spirit essence is linked to the mind energy of all life.

The spirit world mind level is one in which many spirits, whose guiding communications have made them more known to us upon earth, have aspired, a level beyond what is called the second death. A strange expression, I know. All it means is that those who have reached this level of consciousness have moved beyond the need to return to physical life upon earth. They have effectively 'died' to the astral as well as the physical dimension; they have sufficiently experienced all earthly lessons and carry no adverse karma. In other words they need not reincarnate again, although, having freewill, they can do so if they so choose. (I can hear the cries "don't do it, you mad fool!").

Beyond mind level is the realm that can justifiably be called the spiritual level. Greater knowledge and higher truths are naturally available to those who aspire to reach the spiritual realm. Indeed, this is so at each level. However, at this level we are in a sense moving further away from earth life, to a level where the pursuit of philosophy, to give it a familiar title and greater knowledge and understanding of creation, is a natural desire. Once again the desire to serve in some way is, I am quite sure, the norm. Many from this level act as guides to those in the mind level, and will happily impart knowledge of the wisdom they have gathered. This, when appropriate will, in turn, be passed downwards. On occasions they may also bring wisdom and healing energies directly to those upon earth, but more generally this will be passed via intermediaries. So in one way or perhaps many ways, they seek to assist in the progression of those below.

The highest realm is the celestial, although even here there are likely to be many sub-levels; for the new arrival at this level cannot hope to have the wisdom of the more progressed sages.

The celestial is a level that many would equate with spiritual masters. Those who may take some responsibility in formulating suitable re-birth and other plans for those below. Although I do not personally care for the title "master" being used for anyone, for in essence we are all equal, although some have progressed to higher levels of consciousness. It is most difficult when using our earthly language to find adequate terms, those, which suitably convey an understanding of such positions without them sounding hierarchical.

Many people do not let this fact concern them and happily use these terms and in one sense, of course, they are totally justified in doing so. Provided their readers or students realise that no hierarchical system of domination exists within the realms. Those in higher realms do not dominate those below in any way, shape or form. They are merely the custodians of certain wisdom (that, when we reach the right level will be open to us), and by using it wisely they seek to guide, advise and help in numerous ways. They are aware of our needs; of the experiences we need to encounter to further our spiritual progression. They have trodden the same pathway themselves, perhaps many thousands of years previous, we should be pleased to receive their help, for spiritually they are much further ahead of us than we physically are of a new born baby. We would not dream of leaving a newly born baby to care for his or herself, it would be a crime, and our common sense tells us that they would physically perish. In the same way, those from the celestial realm do not sit idle watching us make the same mistakes over and over again, like a loving parent they at least try to guide, although since we have freewill it is still our choice to listen or ignore.

How does guidance from the celestial level reach us? Once more, it tends to come down through intermediary guides and helpers at each level. So guidance from the celestial may in chain fashion be passed down via guides at each appropriate level, spiritual, mind, or astral, according to our personal level of understanding and which guide can attune to our level of vibration. When it reaches us, other than through books and via mediums, the desired guidance will generally do so via our subconscious mind, from where it will filter into our thoughts via our intuitive thinking processes. The vast majority of us do not realise this, thinking that ideas that suddenly formulate, or pop in to our mind are purely of our own making. Often this is not so, but because it appears so natural to us, and happens so regularly throughout our lifetime, that it seems no one else is involved.

As instantly as they might arrive, such subtly communicated thoughts are unfortunately all too easily dismissed, for they do not impinge upon our freewill choice, they are guiding-thoughts only if we allow them to be so. The indoctrinated religious, scientific, material, social and family programming, for the majority, is all too powerful to allow them entry for proper evaluation. This encourages us to dismiss as imagination anything outside of the perceived parameters of 'normal' or 'conventional'. From childhood, even as babies, we are brought into line with what is considered acceptable. Sometimes this is reasonable, for instance to prevent physical harm but all too soon it reaches in to impinge upon mind and poisons us to spiritual reality. It denies us the true facts of life eternal, for our earthly teachers are mostly ignorant of them. We become the blind led by the blind. Further and further we travel down the material cul-de-sacs of spiritual frustration. Only the lucky few are able to free themselves totally from the boundaries imposed by earthly misinformation. To reach the spiritual wisdom located over the rainbow. Perhaps you are one such being? If so, I offer you my humble, heartfelt congratulations.

CONCLUSION

It is only the physical form that perishes at the end of our earthly years. The spirit is eternal and indestructible. It is capable of changing form, as with reincarnation and its progression from the most humble of divine sparks through to human. When it progresses beyond the need to return to earth and further through the spirit realms it will eventually change form again. All will be in accordance with individual progression and natural law and undoubtedly, like growing from children to adults, will at the time seem perfectly normal for us.

Other than clairvoyantly or through materialisation, spirit people or animals are not seen upon earth because their rate of vibration is faster than the speed of light and therefore, beyond the optical range of our physical eyes. Yet they are there - around us and with us on many occasions, as their communications prove.

Communication is not straightforward or easy. It requires a medium, whether mental, trance, physical, or artistic, for it is inter-dimensional communication. We should personally 'test the spirits' or the mediums, and not take everything they may say without consideration and deliberation. Since whether in spirit or upon earth we are all far from perfection. We should however, be open-minded enough to for ourselves judge fairly; and when we do, survival can undoubtedly be proven to us by communication. Understanding that life is eternal is then unquestionably ours.

Ultimately, of even greater importance than knowledge of survival, is awareness of the natural laws, principally, *cause and effect*. For coupled with survival and reincarnation, our understanding of this is so vital. Our immediate and eternal future is dictated by how we live here and now, for at all times do our thoughts, actions and reactions reverberate back to us. We each have freewill. So whether we take notice of this knowledge is entirely our own concern.

My task within has been to present you with my understanding to date, I hope that I have adequately done so.

May the love of spirit, the love of life, and the love of creation go with you.

GLOSSARY

Aura or Energy Fields

Around the physical form, as can partially be viewed by certain photographic techniques, is what is often called an aura, or an auric field. In its fullest sense this is considered to be a sevenfold energy field (or seven bodies of energy). Each layer interconnecting with the preceding and following as the field extends outwards, each representative of progressively higher aspects of consciousness.

Ectoplasm

A spirit 'substance' that can be drawn from some (perhaps all) physical mediums is called ectoplasm. This can be 'moulded' by spirit communicators to produce physical matter or form. It has typically been used to allow a spirit communicator to mould a body identical to their physical earthly form.

Overshadowing

Spirit 'overshadowing' typically refers to a medium delivering a talk termed 'inspired'. When the thoughts of the spirit person are telepathically transmitted to the medium as they speak; if all is functioning well the communicated thoughts will be spoken near word perfect. 'Overshadowing' might also be an indication that trance development is possible.

Chakras

We each have seven chakras. These connect with each of the seven energy fields, and with seven glandular systems within the physical body. The chakras are also known as energy centres (or vortices), it is through them that spiritual life-force energy flows.

Meridian Pathways

These are the spirit equivalent of veins and arteries, used for the flow of life-force energy. They are located throughout the physical body, as well as passing from glands and through organs. They have been particularly well documented and used by Acupuncturists.

Life-force energy

To the spirit this is the equivalent of sustenance, enabling it to maintain a healthy link with the physical body. In some cultures it is known as Prana and in others as Chi.

Higher Mind

Part of the aura or energy field represents higher levels of consciousness. The fifth field (or body) onward is known sometimes as the higher mind, because it is beyond or above our normal conscious mind and senses.

Collective Unconscious or Collective Consciousness

At a higher level of life the composite of our earthly consciousness and higher mind is linked together with that of all others. This is often called the collective unconscious. When we are in any way collectively manifesting this, such as when we all want the same thing, this is displaying or using collective consciousness.

A Reading or Sitting

To have a private 'reading' or 'sitting' is the term psychics and mediums often use to describe a private 'consultation'. Although it is also possible to receive a 'reading', meaning a 'message' being passed from someone in spirit, during a public demonstration of mediumship.

A Sensitive

Psychics and mediums can both be called 'sensitives'. For both attune to finer or more 'sensitive' vibrations.

ADDRESSES

Spiritualists' National Union (SNU). The SNU maintain a 'Voluntary Exponents Register' of reputable speakers, platform demonstrators and private sitting mediums. Their registered address is: Redwoods, Stansted Hall, Stansted, Essex, CM24 8UD, UK. Telephone 01279 816363 Website: www.snu.org.uk (same address for The Arthur Findlay College Bookshop).

Psychic News (Weekly Spiritualist & Paranormal Paper). The Coach House, Stansted Hall, Stansted, Essex, CM24 8UD, UK. Telephone 01279 817050

Psychic World Publishing Co. Ltd., (Monthly Independent Spiritualist Paper). PO Box 14, Greenford, Middlesex, UB6 0UF, UK.

Two Worlds (Spiritualism's 68-page monthly magazine). A3 Riverside, Metropolitan Wharf, Wapping Wall, London, E1W 3SS, UK. Telephone 020-7481 4332

"The Seeker" Publications (Quarterly Magazine). Editor, Ken Alexander, "Badgers Brook" 4 Brook Edge, Moor Lane, Brighstone, I.O.W., PO30 4DP, UK.

Circle of Light (Quarterly Booklet). Editor, Dorothy Davies, 32 Church Lane, Ryde, I.O.W., PO33 2NB, UK.

The Spirit Messenger (TSM) Independent Spirit/Psychic Monthly News Magazine, mostly E. London/Essex. Editor, Raye Edwina Brown, 26 Valentine Way, Silver End, Witham, Essex, CM8 3RY, UK.